Epic Vegan

PRESSURE COOKING

Simple Oil-Free Vegan
Pressure Cooker Recipes

HANNAH HOWLETT & DEREK HOWLETT

EPIC VEGAN PRESSURE COOKING

© Hannah Howlett & Derek Howlett 2016

All Rights Reserved. No part of this book may be used or reproduced in any manner whatsoever without written permission.

ISBN# 978-1985202696

Instant Pot® is the registered trademark of Double Insight Inc., and the Instant Pot® was designed in Canada, with healthy living, green living, and ethnic diversity in mind.

    The ideas, concepts and opinions expressed in 'Epic Vegan Pressure Cooking' and recipes are intended to be used for educational purposes only. The books and recipes are sold with the understanding that authors and publisher are not rendering medical advice of any kind, nor are the books or recipes intended to replace medical advice, nor to diagnose, prescribe or treat any disease, condition, illness or injury.

    It is imperative that before beginning any diet or exercise program, including any aspect of the 'Epic Vegan Instant Pot® Cooking' program, you receive full medical clearance from a licensed physician.

    Authors and publisher claim no responsibility to any person or entity for any liability, loss, or damage caused or alleged to be caused directly or indirectly as a result of the use, application or interpretation of the material in the books or recipe guide.

TABLE OF CONTENTS

Information

Why A Pressure Cooker? 7
Why Is This Book Vegan? 9
Accessory Recommendations 11
How To Use A Pressure Cooker 13
Ingredients We Use 15

Recipes

Perfect Rice 21
Perfectly Steamed Potatoes 23
Curry In A Hurry 25
Omg Berry Oatmeal 27
Dman's Epic Refried Beans 29
Bomb.com Corn Chowdahhh 31
No Farts Triple Bean Chili 33
Protein Lentil Stew 35
Texas Cowboy Caviar 37
One Pot Pasta Brah! 39
Mango Sticky Rice 41
Carrot Potato Soup 43
Humdinger Hummus 45
Black Bean Soup Of Glory 47
No Oil Marinara Sauce 49
Veggie Lentil Soup A Looop 51
It's Coming Out Hot Sriracha 53
The Sloppiest Joe (You'll Ever Know) 55
Bomb Diggity Black Bean Rice 57
Dal, Dhal or Dahl? 59
Split 'Em Up Pea Soup 61
Nacho Mom's Hot Dogs 63
Creamy Alfredo Pasta 65
Smashed Potatoes 67
Cheesy Potato Broccoli Soup 69
Pumpkin Steel Cut Oats 71
Amazing Aloo Gobi 73
Carrot Potato Gravy 75
The Black Eyed Peas Chili 77
Asian Style Quinoa 79

The 7 Day Challenge

Why Do This Challenge? 82
Shopping Guide 83
Let's Do This!! 84

Cooking Charts

Rice & Grains 90
Dry Beans & Legumes 91
Fresh Vegetables 92

Resources

Our Other Books 95

INFORMATION

(START HERE AND LEARN ALL OF OUR BEST TIPS & TRICKS)

WHY A PRESSURE COOKER?

When God made lazy people, he also blessed us with the electric pressure cooker at the same time. We aren't religious people at all but we see the electric pressure cooker as some type of voodoo divine creation. We can't really explain it.

We love great tasting food. We also love healthy vegan food. What we really love though is, healthy food that tastes amazing and can be done with a fraction of the effort and in a fraction of the time. This is where an electric pressure cooker fits in. It satisfies all those desires.

It speeds up the cooking time by cooking under pressure. We really don't know how that works but it does. You can do all kinds of meals in under 30 minutes that could take hours in the crockpot or on the stove top. That also means there is a lot less energy used as it is a more efficient cooking method. You can call yourself an enviromentalist now! Woot woot!

The electric pressure cooker is a tool that can help you create delicious batches of healthy, low-fat, plant-based food for you and your family. It can give even the most inept person in the kitchen the ability to create satisfying meals. Ya we used the word 'inept'... whatever.

Why is this important? A lot of us like to believe we are way too busy to make healthy food. Some people are (a lot of us aren't) and we are essentially just lazy when it comes to making really good food. Sometimes that dollar menu is hard to turn down but the dollar menu makes you feel like crap.

We've solved all your problems though. You can still be lazy and eat healthy vegan food. What's even better is because you're cooking big batches of food at once, you can store all of this deliciousness in the fridge and create simple healthy meals on the fly.

Sometimes you get home from work and all you want to do is watch some Hoarders and feel good in knowing that you aren't surrounded by piles of garbage. You're busy and you ain't got time for cooking! No worries, you happened to make buckets of 'Curry In A Hurry' the other night and you've

∽ WHY A PRESSURE COOKER? ∽

got leftovers. BOOOOOM! You're winning at life.

We know some of you are extra lazy and we mustered up the motivation (between Hoarders episodes) to make a little 7 day challenge. We tell you what to make when, so you'll always have some delcious meals ready.

Ok, well we hope you understand why you should be pressure cooking… is that really gonna be a thing now? "Pressure Cooking"!?!? Ya, you know what, we're gonna make it a thing.

Pressure cooking is great and in the next chapter, we will talk about exactly why this recipe book is all plant-based.

WHY IS THIS BOOK VEGAN?

We have both been eating a plant-based vegan diet for a combined 12+ years. We have experienced a number of health improvements plus there are a myriad of environmental benefits and ethical reasons to eat plant-based.

Hannah has lost over 70 lbs by following a plant-based diet and has successfully gotten over addictions to cigarettes, adderall and alcohol. Derek has lost 20 lbs, healed really painful cystic acne and has cycle toured around Vietnam, Cambodia, Thailand, Malaysia and Australia all while eating vegan.

We both know that a whole food plant-based diet works in our lives but it also works for millions around the world. It has helped people reverse many common day health diseases. We aren't medical doctors and can't tell you if it will help you or not but we do believe it does have powerful healing properties.

We follow a starch-based vegan diet that has gained massive popularity through Dr. John McDougall, who is our biggest hero. Dr. McDougall has helped tens of thousands of people through his books and programs to regain their health and lose excess body weight for good.

John made the simple but profound observation, "All large populations of trim, healthy people, throughout verifiable human history, have obtained the bulk of their calories from starch."

And that is what this recipe book is all about. Giving you the recipes, tools and tips to get the bulk of your calories from starches like potatoes, rice, lentils, corn, oatmeal and quinoa. Mix in some fruits, vegetables and you've got a very well rounded diet that can improve your health dramatically.

Don't take our word for it though. John McDougall has a list of testimonials on his website that show amazing transformations. https://www.drmcdougall.com/health/education/health-science/stars/

We also highly recommend that you pick up his book, The Starch Solution.

~ WHY IS THIS BOOK VEGAN? ~

It is THE book to read if you are seriously considering eating a plant-based diet for health.

SOME QUICK REASONS TO GO VEGAN AND EAT A WHOLE FOODS PLANT-BASED DIET:

FOR YOUR HEALTH

Following a healthy, balanced vegan diet ensures a number health benefits. It can also prevent and possibly reverse some of our most common diseases that are killing us by the hundreds of thousands every year.

Most vegans are not just your typical woo-woo hippy type as some would lead you to believe. They can be people who are passionate about living a high energy life and getting things done in their life. Eating a vegan diet low in fat and junk food gives them the energy and vitality to really live their life.

FOR THE PLANET

Up to 51% of global greenhouse gas emissions is due to livestock and their by products. The meat and dairy industry use 1/3 of the earths fresh water. Animal agriculture is responsible for 91% of the Amazon rainforest destruction. 90 million tons of fish are pulled from the oceans every year.

1 1/2 acres of land could produce 375lbs of meat or 37,000lbs of plant-based food. Animal agriculture is the leading cause of species extinction, ocean dead zones, water pollution and habitat destruction. Being vegan is a big deal in a world where the environment is being destroyed.

FOR THE ANIMALS

There is no such thing as 'humane' slaughter. Slaughter is slaughter. Animals are held in horrific conditions from birth till death. Animals in the agriculture business are seen as a commodity, not as sentient beings. Why eat a pig but love your dog? They both have the same relative intelligence.

MORE RESOURCES

Books: The China Study, Prevent and Reverse Heart Disease, How Not To Die, The Starch Solution, Dr. Neal Barnard's Program For Reversing Diabetes

DVDs: Forks Over Knives, Cowspiracy, Earthlings

ACCESSORY RECOMMENDATIONS

Alright, so you buy your first car and you're all excited. It looks great, you're feeling like a champ and you drive it around town with the music pumping.

Sounds like a perfect story... but is it? What if you threw on some spinners, tinted the windows and installed some under car lighting. It would be looking pretty fly. Sure... you'd get some haters but honestly... accessorize anyways!

It's the same with your pressure cooker. The standalone product is great but throw in a few accessories and you'll be pressure cooking like a BOSS!

The first thing we recommend is getting a second inner pot. It's really handy when you want to cook meals back to back. You can have the next pot ready to cook before the first one is even finished. Plus, it can be a bit of a pain in the butt to always have to transfer leftovers to tupperware containers.

The next blingin' accessory are some silicone cover lids. The silicon lids we recommend can cover your inner pots when you have them stored away in the fridge. This keeps your leftovers super fresh.

The last thing we recommend is an immersion blender. These little hand blenders are awesome for blending up soups right in your pressure cooker. No need to put it in your Vitamix.

Here are some links to what we recommend (these are affiliate links so those rich dudes at Amazon send us a few bucks for making them millionaires)

- Instant Pot® Duo Mini 3 qt
- Extra Inner Pots
- Silicone Cover Lids
- Immersion Blender (Hand Blender)

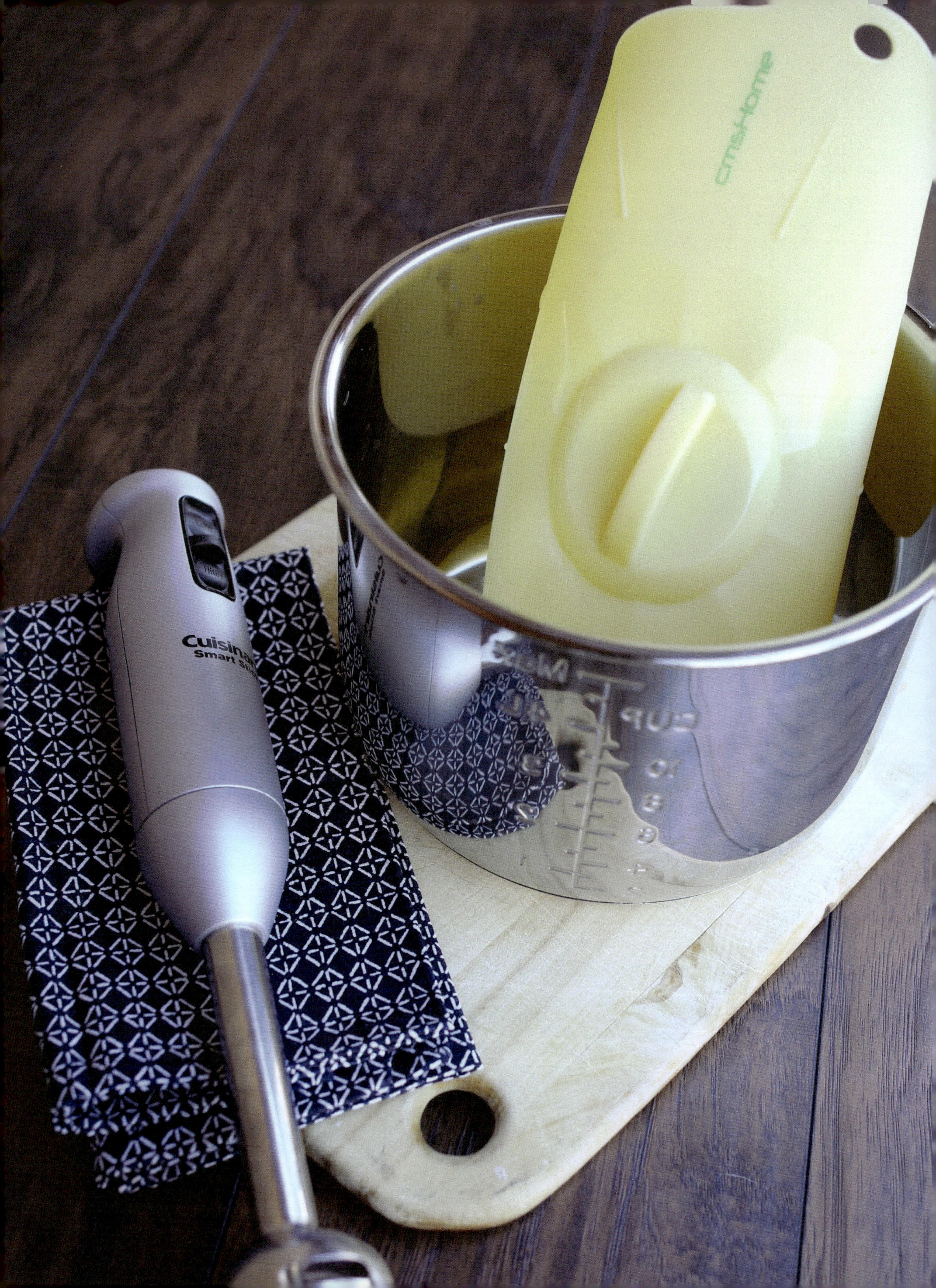
cmsHome
CUP

HOW TO USE A PRESSURE COOKER

The Instant Pot® has got a lot of fancy buttons on it and it can seem a little daunting. No worries though because we are only going to use a few of them. We have the Instant Pot® Duo Mini 3 qt. There aren't any important features that our Instant Pot® has that your pressure cooker won't.

All of the important safety instructions should be consulted in the Instant Pot® user manual. We aren't going to give you any safety instructions cause we don't like getting mixed up with lawyers.

3 MOST IMPORTANT FUNCTION KEYS WE USE

The main button that we use for cooking is the 'Pressure Cook' button. When you hit it, the number 30 pops up (for 30 minutes) then you adjust the time with the plus and minus buttons. This represents the cooking time once the Instant Pot® comes to pressure. This can be misleading because in the iPot recipe book it says that it only takes 4 minutes to cook rice but what they don't really say is that the iPot needs 5-8 minutes to come to pressure and you should do a 10 minute natural steam release. So in reality the cooking time is at least 20 minutes. It's still really fast but the cooking times can be misleading.

The 'Keep Warm' button is pretty self-explanatory. When the Instant Pot® is cooking from the pressure cook setting it automatically switches to 'Keep Warm' when the cooking time elapses. In order to switch the iPot to a standby mode, hit this button. If it's in a standby mode and you want it to 'Keep Warm', just hit the button. If you fudge up the cooking time when setting the iPot, no worries! Just hit the cancel button and you can try again.

The next button we like to use is the 'Sautée' button for open lid sautéing. There are three settings for this button: low, medium and hot. It goes to normal by default. For some of the recipes we may ask you to sautée some garlic or onions up beforehand. Sautéing releases the flavors trapped inside. Where are those flavors trapped? We have no idea. You have to ask the onions, garlic and peppers for more details about that.

～ HOW TO USE A PRESSURE COOKER ～

PRESSURE RELEASE METHODS

On the top of the Instant Pot® is a steam release handle. For every recipe you will want this pointed towards 'sealing'. This seals the Instant Pot® so it builds up pressure and reduces overall cooking time. You can also move it towards 'venting' and that allows any built up steam to safely release.

There are different ways to release the pressure so let's go over those. It's important to let the cooking cycle finish. This is noted when your iPot starts beeping like cray cray.

QUICK RELEASE

When the cooking cycle has finished, hit the cancel button and switch the steam release handle to 'venting'. BE CAREFUL!! Lots of hot steam will be released so keep your face away from the handle. Also make sure you don't pull the release handle off of the iPot. Things could get really scary.

Quick release isn't for food in large liquid volume or with high starch content (porridge, rice, sticky liquids, soup, etc). The food can splatter out with the steam.

NATURAL RELEASE

This release method is when you let the cooker cool down nautrally until the float valve drops down (that's the silver thing next to the steam release handle). Depending on how much food is in the iPot, it can take between 10-30 minutes (sometimes longer) for this to happen when the cooker is in the 'Keep-Warm' mode.

10 MINUTE RELEASE

We use this method quite often. After the cooker has finished its cooking cycle and moves in to the 'Keep-Warm' mode, wait 10 minutes, hit the 'Cancel' button then move the release handle to 'venting'.

We will set a timer on our cell phone to 10 minutes when we hear the iPot beeping (when the cooking cycle has finished) so we know exactly when the 10 minutes is up. Just a handy dandy tip.

The different release methods control how long the food is going to be cooked for and in what way.

INGREDIENTS WE USE

For the vast majority of this recipe book, we use whole plant-based foods and common spices. There are some recipes that call for certain products or ingredients that are less common. We did this because these products are economical and can save you a lot of time in the kitchen. We know you can be lazy so we try to make things as easy as possible to create really delicious meals.

If you live in Canada or the U.S.A. all of these products should be easy to find. In other countries around the world they may be more difficult. We will list the specific products we used along with the ingredients and a picture so you can find a similar replacement.

We know how frustrating it can be in recipe books when they include certain ingredients and you're thinking… "what the heck is that!?!?" We want to make this as easy as possible for you. That way you're happy and you won't leave us a nasty review on Amazon. Not that you would do it that right? This way everybody wins! Wooop wooop!

MEXICAN TOMATO SAUCE

This is a sauce that is normally used for tacos and enchiladas but it made a great addition to our Cowboy Caviar recipe. Look for it in the Mexican or Hispanic section of your grocery store. The brand is 'El Pato' and comes in a 7 3/4 oz (220g) tin can.

INGREDIENTS: tomato purée, water, chiles, onions, garlic, salt and spices.

MEXICAN SALSA

Most salsa is usually a little chunkier but this salsa is really thin. It works great in our refried beans to thin out the recipe. This is very flavorful and has a great punch to it. The brand is 'Herdez' and comes in a 7 oz (198g) tin can.

INGREDIENTS: tomatoes, onion, serrano peppers, iodized salt and cilantro.

~ INGREDIENTS WE USE ~

BETTER THAN BOUILLON

This is one of those economical purchases that just makes sense. One jar of BTB which is 8 oz, equates to 9.5 quarts (or litres) of vegetable broth. 1 tsp of BTB is the equivalent to one bouillon cube and 1 1/2 tbsp of BTB is equivalent to 1 quart of veggie broth.

So in this recipe book, if the recipe calls for 2 cups of vegetable broth, you can subsitute it with 2 cups of water and 2 tsp of BTB. Super handy! Yes, there is a tiny amount of oil in the BTB but it's such a minor amount. If you are worried about it, just use oil-free veggie broth instead.

INGREDIENTS: vegetables and concentrated vegetable juices (carrots, celery, onion, tomato, onion*, potato*, garlic*) hydrolyzed soy protein, salt, yeast extract, sugar, maltodextrin (from corn), soybean oil, spice extractive. *dehydrated.

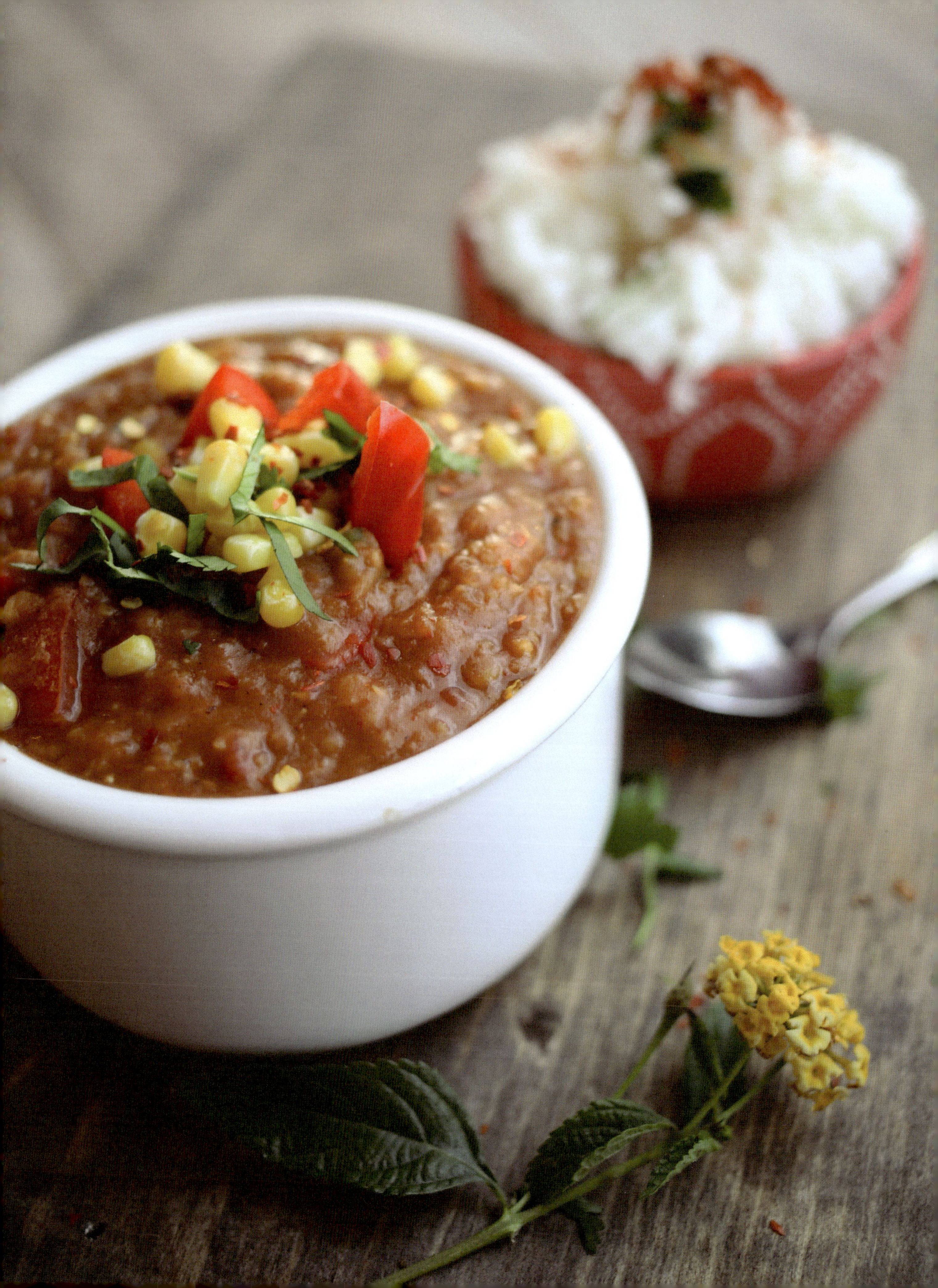

RECIPES

(THIS IS WHERE THE GOOD STUFF IS)

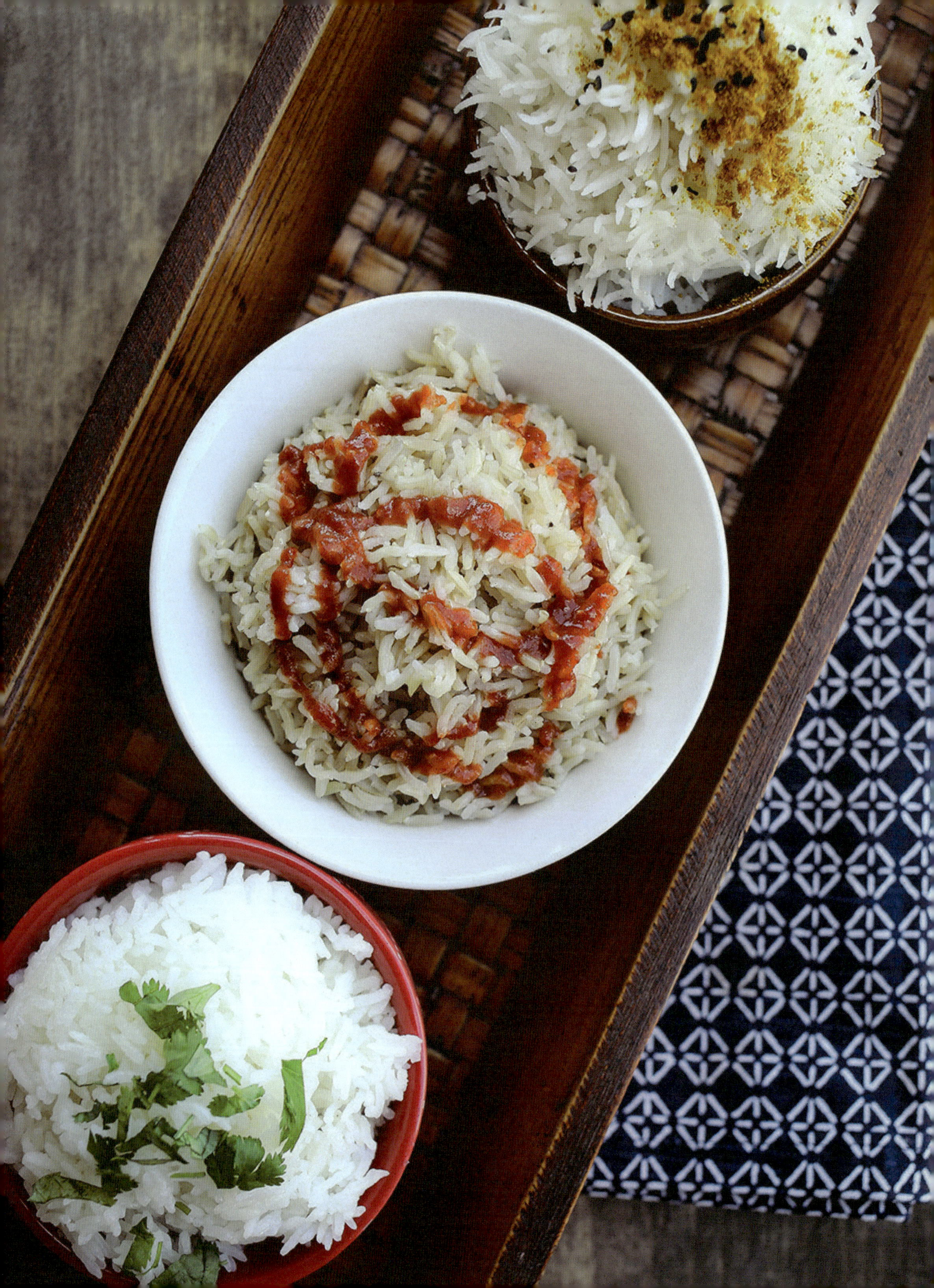

PERFECT RICE

Did you know your blinging iPot can be used to make some bomb diggity rice?? Oh you better believe it! Rice is the base for most of our meals so we love perfect rice every single time.

INGREDIENTS

JASMINE RICE (1:1 RATIO)
- 3 cups of jasmine rice
- 3 cups of water

BASMATI RICE (1:1.5 RATIO)
- 2 cups of basmati rice
- 3 cups of water

BROWN RICE (1:1.25 RATIO)
- 2 cups of brown rice
- 2 1/2 cups of water

Cooking perfect rice works in ratios. So if you have 1 cup of jasmine rice, you will use 1 cup of water for it. There are different ratios for different styles of rice that are noted above.

***Keep in mind that these ratios are different from cooking on the stove top.

METHOD

When you select the amount of rice you want to cook, quickly rinse it using a fine mesh strainer. Add it to your Instant Pot® followed by the amount of water required.

Close up your Instant Pot® and make sure to set the steam release handle on the lid to 'sealing'.

Hit the pressure cook button, leave on high pressure and the cook times are:

Jasmine Rice - 4 minutes
Basmati Rice - 4 minutes
Any Brown Rice - 22 minutes

Just set it and forget it! The iPot will beep a bunch of times when it is done cooking. Let the iPot naturally release steam for 10 minutes.

After the 10 minutes is up, switch the steam release handle to 'venting'. Once the steam is released, enjoy your rice with any of the stews, soups and chilis in this book!

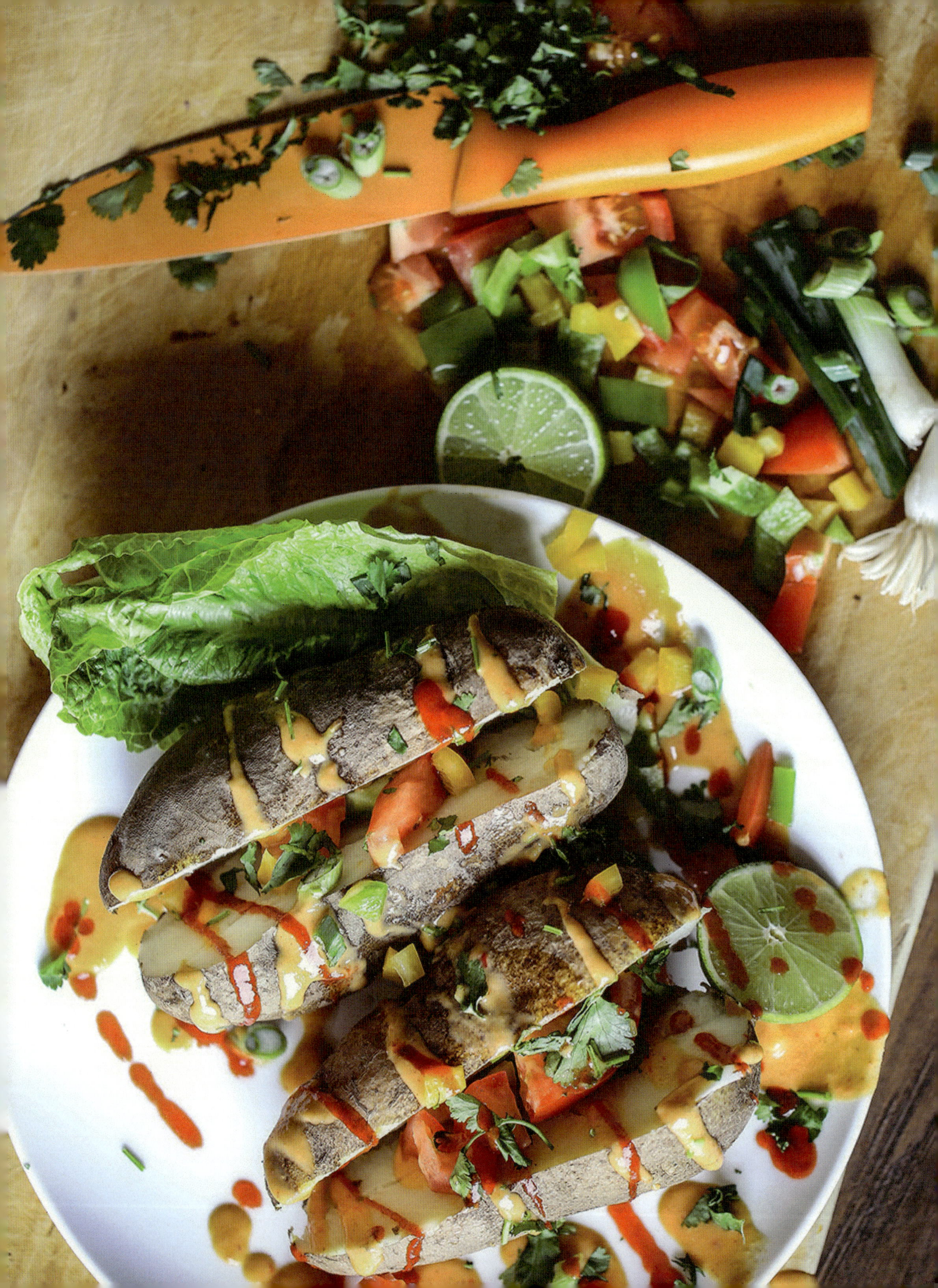

PERFECTLY STEAMED POTATOES

Along with the perfect rice recipe above, we love perfectly steamed potatoes. They are great for weight loss as they are low in caloric density and also very satiating.

SERVINGS	PREP TIME	TOTAL COOK TIME
As many as you want	10 minutes	25-35 minutes

INGREDIENTS

Whole potatoes, any kind

GARNISH
Tomato
Sweet peppers
Cilantro
Green onion

SAUCES
Potato nacho sauce**
Sriracha

**For the nacho sauce recipe used in the photo, go to:
https://highcarbhannah.co/recipes/badass-vegan-nachos/

METHOD

Wash and scrub your potatoes clean. Insert the trivet (metal rack that comes with your Instant Pot) in to the Instant Pot and add in 2 cups of water. Insert your whole potatoes directly on the trivet rack and put the cover on.

Hit the pressure cook button and set the time according to the size of potatoes you have. If you're unsure of what time to use, choose more time to ensure the potatoes are cooked all the way through.

Large - 15 minutes
Medium - 12 minutes
Small - 10 minutes.

Make sure the steam release handle is set to 'sealing'. Once the cooking time is up, let the potatoes naturally release for at least 10 minutes. Switch the handle to 'venting' to release any extra steam and remove the cover lid.

Put whatever delectables you enjoy on top and devour some potato carbness.

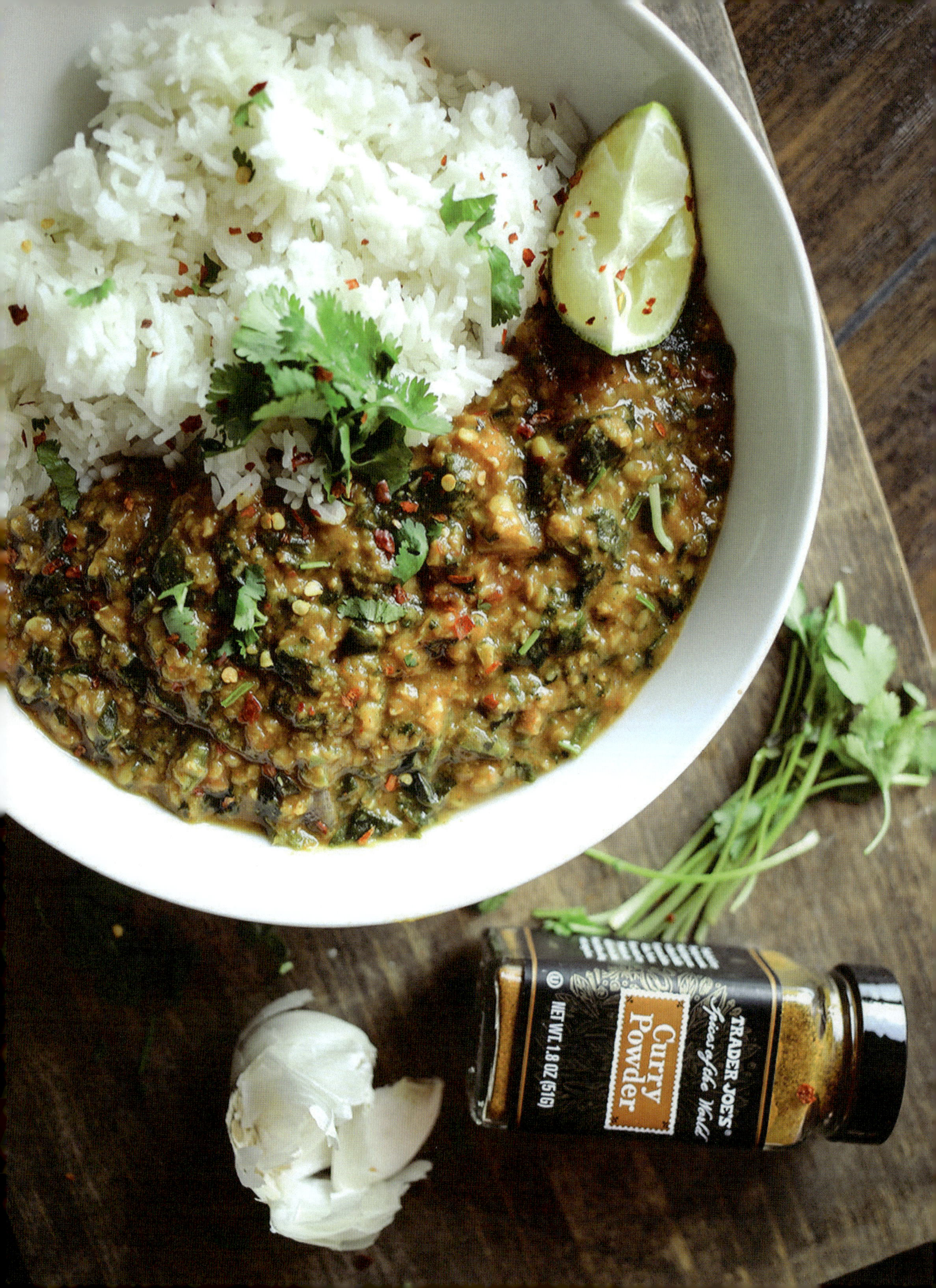
TRADER JOE'S
Spices of the World
Curry Powder
NET WT. 1.8 OZ (51G)

CURRY IN A HURRY

A lot of people love curry. Ya... that's great and all but what if you're in a hurry? We need this done real quick and your Instant Pot® will help you speed it up way quicker.

SERVINGS	PREP TIME	TOTAL COOK TIME
3 x 570 calories servings	10 minutes	25 minutes

INGREDIENTS

- 1 can (13.5 fl oz or 400mL) of light coconut milk
- 1 can (14.5 fl oz or 429mL) of diced tomatoes
- 2 cups of red lentils
- 3 tbsp of tomato paste
- 1 red onion, chopped
- 3 cloves of garlic, minced
- 5 cups of water
- 2 tsp of Better Than Bouillon Vegetable Base**
- 2 tbsp curry powder
- 1 tsp of cayenne pepper
- 1 cup of chopped frozen spinach

**'Better Than Bouillon Vegetable Base' is a concentrated base of dehydrated veggies used to add more flavor to stews and soups.

If you don't have access to this, you can substitute some of the cups of water with cups of veggie broth. You could use 2 cups of veggie broth with 3 cups of water for this recipe.

METHOD

Ok, we're gonna keep this one real simple.

Prepare the garlic and red onion first. Then combine all the ingredients (except for the frozen spinach) directly in to the Instant Pot®.

We like to keep our onions in the fridge and cut them cold. Reduces tears.

Hit the pressure cook button and set the timer to 15 minutes on high pressure. Ensure the steam release handle is set to 'sealing'.

When finished, let the pressure naturally release for 10 minutes then switch the handle to 'venting'.

When you open up the lid, add in the spinach. Stir this very well and serve in 5 minutes.

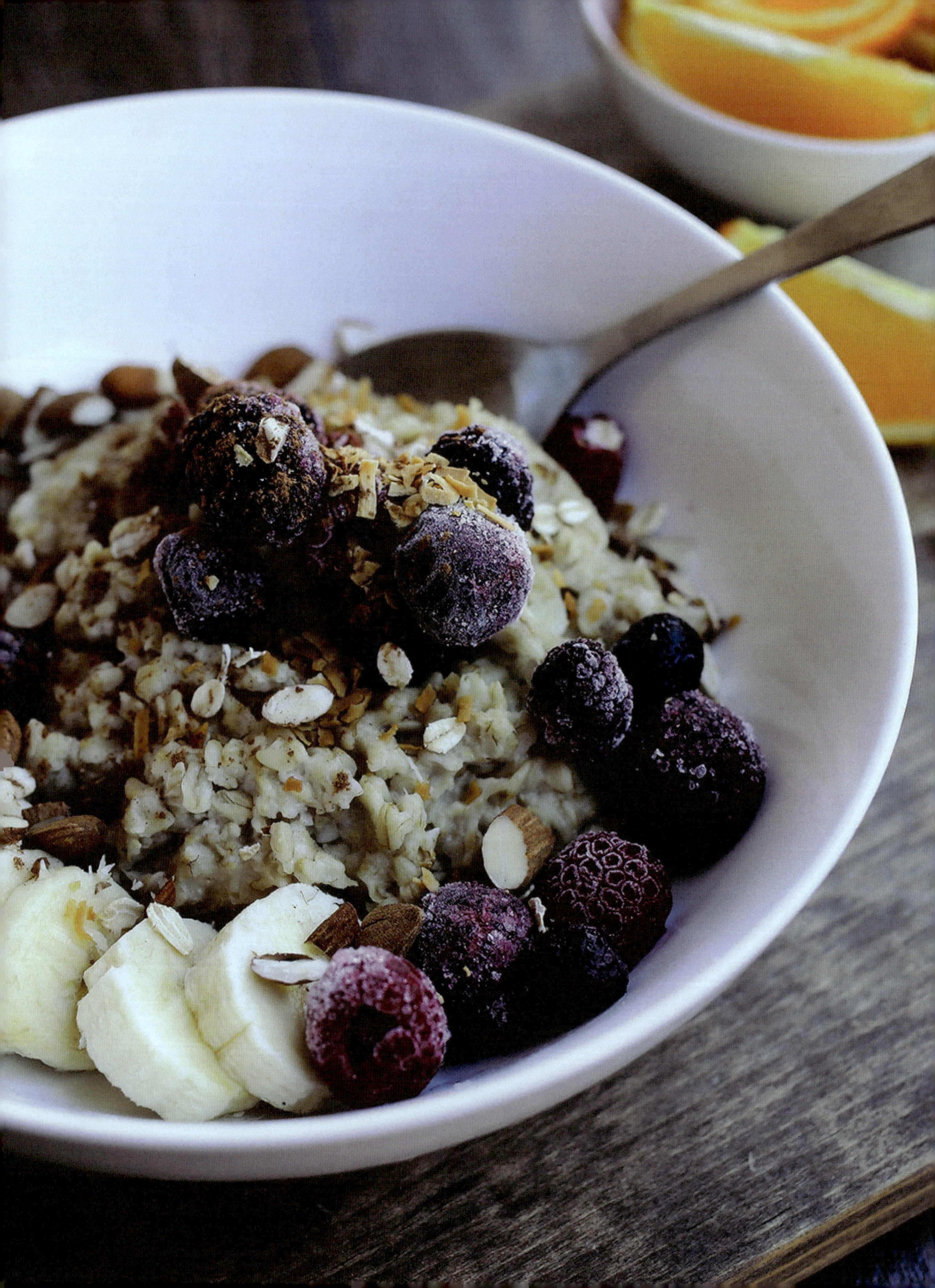

OMG BERRY OATMEAL

You might be thinking... can you do oatmeal in the Instant Pot®? Ya damn right you can do oatmeal in the iPot! Here's a simple breakfast recipe that is a huge humdinger winner!

SERVINGS
1 serving at 570 calories

PREP TIME
5 minutes

TOTAL COOK TIME
25 minutes

INGREDIENTS

OATMEAL (1:1.66 RATIO)

- 1 cup of quick oats
- 1 2/3 cups of water
- 1 cup of frozen berries
- 1 banana, chopped
- 1-2 tbsp of brown sugar
- 1/4 cup soy milk or almond milk

Oatmeal can be very finicky with the cooking time and ratio of oatmeal to water so if your first batch comes out like crap, keep trying till it comes out perfect but this ratio should work really well!

GARNISH (OPTIONAL)
Chopped almonds
Coconut flakes

METHOD

Measure out your oats and water. Place both of them directly in to your Instant Pot®. Put the cover on.

Set the iPot on pressure cook for 6 minutes on high pressure and when the timer finishes let it naturally release pressure for 10 minutes or so. After 10 minutes, switch the steam release handle to 'venting' to release the remaining steam. Open the lid.

When the oats are done, place in to a bowl and top with the mixed berries, chopped banana, sugar and non-dairy milk and you'll be absolutely rocking!!

1 cup of oats might not be enough for you or for who you're making it for. Just multiply the amount of oats and water and maintain the same ratio for perfect oatmeal!

✳✳✳
D's Epic Tip

Place one frozen banana in to the iPot when you're cooking your oatmeal and mix it around when it's finished for a super creamy oatmeal.

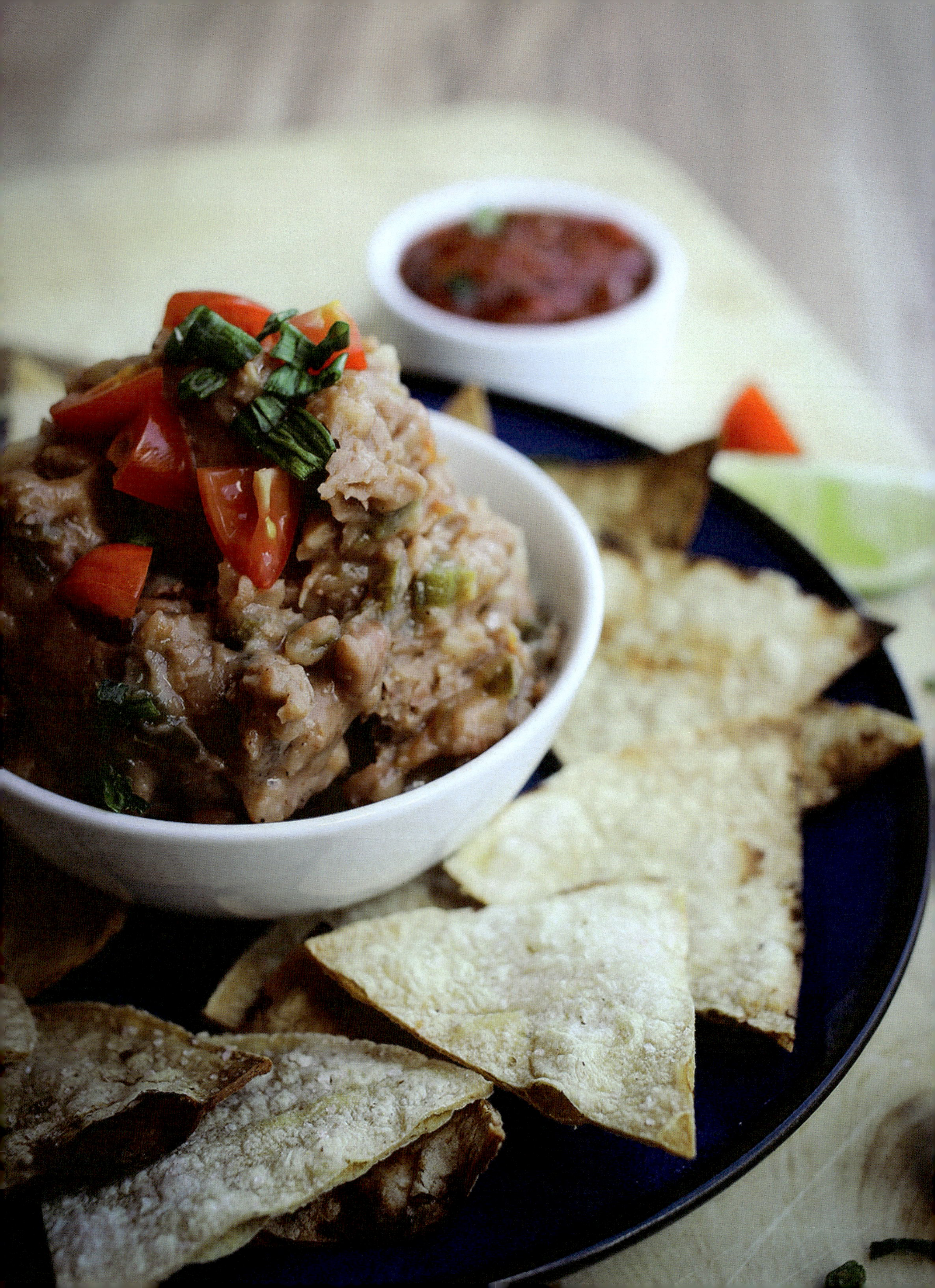

DMAN'S EPIC REFRIED BEANS

Refried beans are a staple in our household. We love making a big batch of them so that we have lots for our burrito bowls. These are way tastier than canned beans. Plus you know everything that is going in to it. win freaking win baby!

SERVINGS	PREP TIME	TOTAL COOK TIME
6 x 150 calorie servings	15 minutes	60 minutes

INGREDIENTS

1 1/2	cups of dry pinto beans
1	tbsp of chili powder
1	tbsp of cumin
1	tsp of your favorite salt
3/4	cups (180mL) of salsa**
4 oz	(80mL) can of diced jalapeños

**For the salsa and the diced jalapeños, we found small tins of them in the Mexican or Hispanic section of the grocery store. For more information on this salsa, check out the 'Ingredients We Use' chapter.

If you can't find these or have access to them, use regular salsa and you could dice some deseeded jalapeño peppers for spice if you can't find the diced jalapeños at your local store.

***The corn chips in the photo are corn tortillas sliced and baked at 400F for 8-10 minutes with lime juice and salt on top.

METHOD

Rinse the beans in a strainer then place in your iPot. Cover with water so that there is about 2 inches (5cm) of water covering the top of the beans.

Set the iPot on pressure cook for 45 minutes at high pressure. Make sure the steam release handle is set to 'sealing'. When the 45 minutes is done cooking, hit the 'Cancel' button and allow the pressure to come down naturally for 10 minutes. Release the remaining steam using the release valve.

Drain the beans in to a strainer and place them in to a bowl or a container you'll be storing them in (you can reserve some of the broth if you want). The beans should be quite soft now. Add in the chili powder, cumin and salt.

You can use an immersion blender, a potato masher or even the back of a fork or spoon to mash the beans to your desired consistency. We like it thick and chunky so we don't mash all the beans.

Add in the salsa and diced jalapeños to your beans and mix with a spoon. If you like your beans a little bit more soupy, then you could reserve some of the bean broth water from when you drained them earlier and mix that in.

TRADER JOE'S
Spices of the World
Smoked Paprika
NET WT. 1.6 OZ (45G)

BOMB.COM CORN CHOWDAHHH

We contacted Bomb.com and asked if we could use their website address to sponsor this recipe... they flat out had no idea what we were talking about. anyways, we hope you love this corn chowdahhh.

SERVINGS	PREP TIME	TOTAL COOK TIME
4 x 600 calorie servings	15 minutes	30 minutes

INGREDIENTS

CHOWDAHHH

- 5 potatoes (1000g or 2 lbs), peeled & chopped
- 3 cups (1 lb or 454g) of fresh or frozen corn
- 3 cloves of garlic, minced
- 1 large red pepper, chopped
- 1 yellow onion, chopped
- 2 tsp smoked paprika (different than regular paprika)
- 2 cups of veggie broth (or you can use 2 cups of water with 2 tsp of 'better than bouillon')
- 1 can (13.5 fl oz or 400mL) of light coconut milk

GARNISH (OPTIONAL)

Salt and black pepper to taste
Chopped green onion, cilantro
Red pepper, corn (reserved from ingredients above)

METHOD

Chop the onion and mince the garlic. Place those in the iPot. Chop up the potatoes and red pepper and leave aside.

Turn your Instant Pot® on to sautée and add about 1/4 to 1/2 cup of broth (or water). Use a long wooden spoon or spatula to stir the onion and garlic while it is sautéing. Do this for 5 minutes then add in the remaining ingredients and spices.

Mix slowly and close the iPot lid. Make sure the vent is set to 'sealing'. Hit the pressure cook button and set the time to 8 minutes on high pressure. When the iPot is finished, do a 10 minute pressure release (explained in the 'How To Use The Instant Pot®' section).

Insert an immersion blender and give it short zaps until the soup thickens up but still has some chunky bits. If you don't have an immersion blender, remove 1/2 of the soup, blend (in a regular blender) and mix it back with the remaining soup in the iPot. Be careful because the soup will be very hot!

Serve the chowdahhh over rice if you desire and garnish with corn, red pepper, cilantro, green onion, salt and pepper.

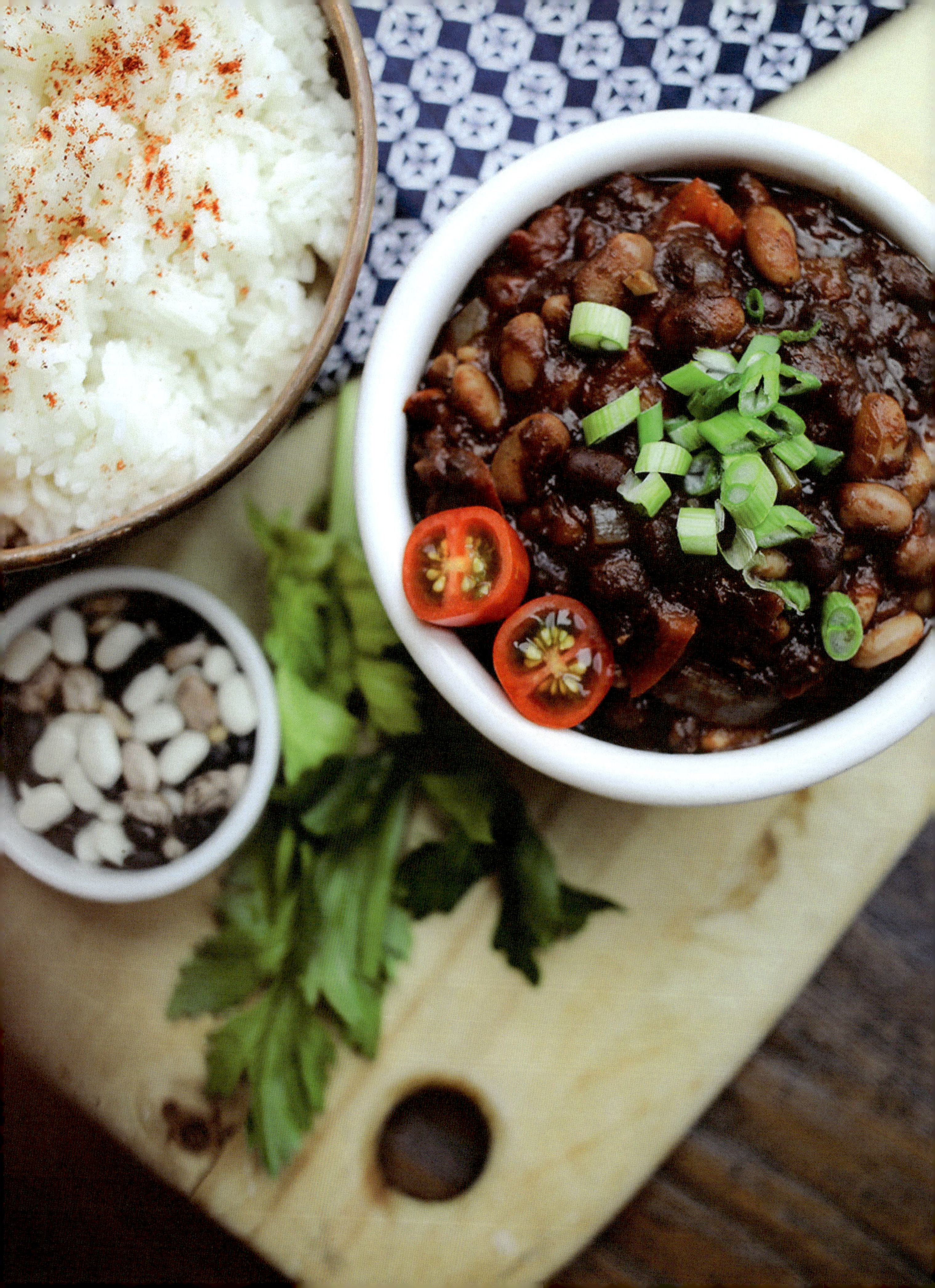

NO FARTS TRIPLE BEAN CHILI

*** *Disclaimer - Hannah and Derek Make no claim that this bean chili will leave you without any farts We honestly just thought that this would be a funny recipe name for a bean chili. Use at your own discretion!!*

SERVINGS
2 x 515 calorie servings

PREP TIME
15 minutes

TOTAL COOK TIME
60 minutes

INGREDIENTS

CHILI

2/3	cup of dry black beans
2/3	cup of dry navy beans
2/3	cup of dry pinto beans
1/4	cup of dry red lentils
1	red bell pepper, chopped
1	can (14.5 fl oz or 429mL) of diced tomoatoes
1	can (6 oz or 170g) of tomato paste
2	tbsp chili powder
1	tbsp ground cumin
3 1/2	cups of water or veggie broth
1	onion (red or yellow), chopped
2	cloves of garlic, minced
2	ribs of celery, chopped

TOPPINGS
Thinly sliced green onion
Nutritional yeast
Himalayan salt

METHOD

Ok... here we go. No farts chili... lol. Mince the garlic and chop the onion. Fill up the iPot with the water or veggie broth. Add in the garlic, 1/2 of the onion, can of diced tomatoes, beans, 1/2 of the bell pepper, tomato paste, red lentils, chili powder and cumin.

Put the lid on the iPot and hit the pressure cook button and set the timer to 32 minutes on high pressure. When finished, let it release steam naturally for 15 minutes. After the 15 minutes is up, switch the steam release handle to 'venting' to release any extra steam.

While the chili is hot, add in the celery and remaining 1/2 onion and 1/2 red pepper. Let it simmer for 10 minutes in the 'Keep Warm' cycle. Then hit the 'Cancel' button and the chili is ready to serve.

***
D's Epic Tip

We like to add salt to our food once it's finished cooking. The taste of the salt dissapates when it is cooking and nobody likes that.

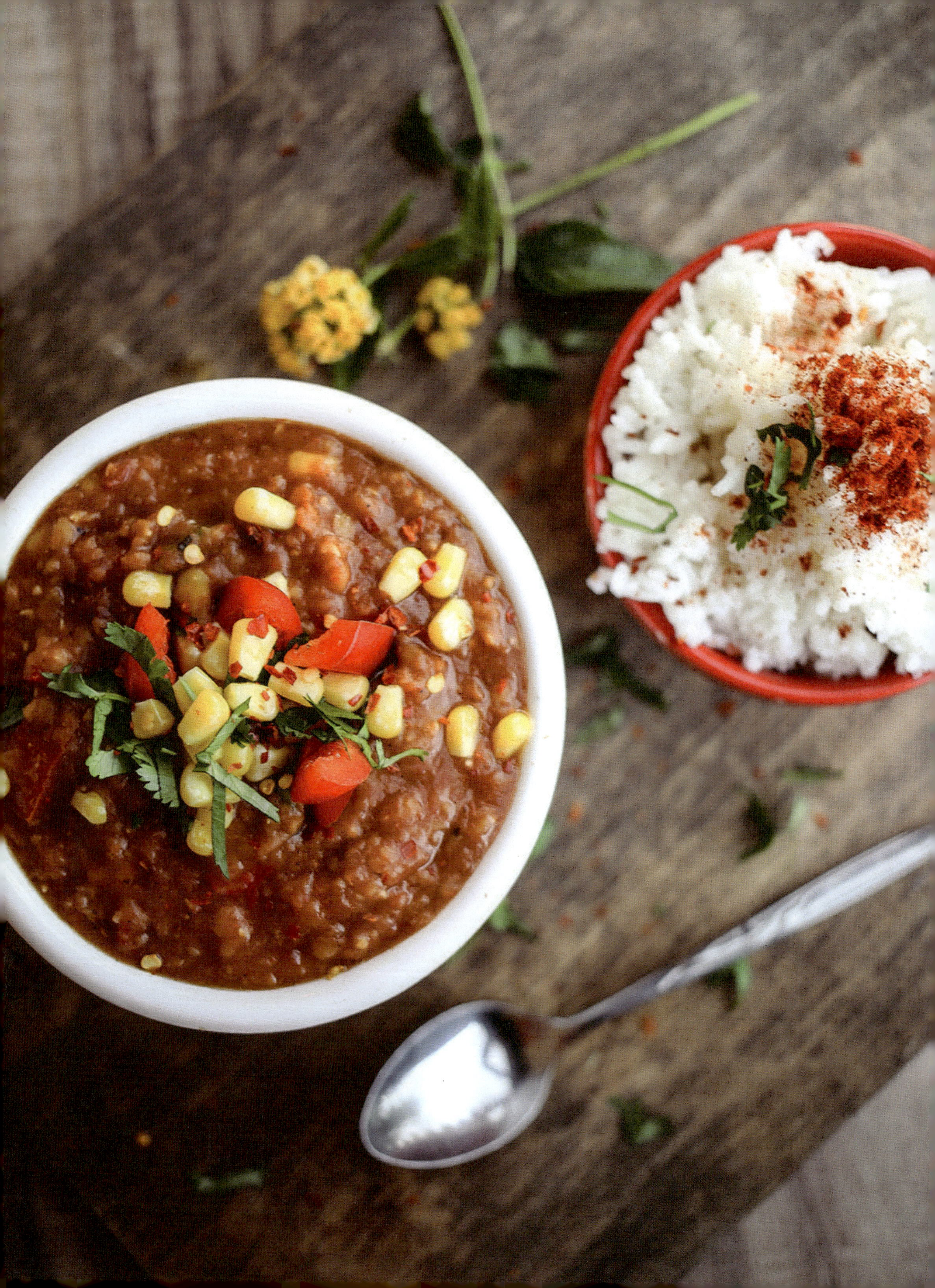

PROTEIN LENTIL STEW

This recipe is for all of the people who think that us vegans can't get protein. Lentils have 33% of their calories coming from protein. Just in this recipe there is over 100 grams of protein from the lentils alone. wooop woooop!!

SERVINGS 3 x 600 calorie servings	**PREP TIME** 10 minutes	**TOTAL COOK TIME** 45 minutes

INGREDIENTS

- 2   cups of dry red lentils *
- 7   cups of water
- 1/4 cup of brown sugar /coconut
- 1   can (14.5 fl oz or 429mL) of diced tomatoes
- 1   can (6 oz or 170g) of tomato paste *Not used*
- 1   tbsp chili powder ✗
- 2   tsp Better Than Bouillon (optional) 1½
- 1   tsp smoked paprika
- 1   tsp of cayenne pepper
- 1   red pepper, diced
- 2   medium sized tomatoes, diced
- 2   ribs of celery, diced
- 1   cup of fresh or frozen corn

Handwritten notes:
Amazing!
* No chili
- 1 cup of lentils
- 2 cups of courgette (half a big one)
- No tom paste
- 1½ tsp stock
- Top with onion, coriander, spring onions

METHOD

You're going to feel really strong after this eating some of this stew! Actually... not. You'll just feel full.

Quickly rinse your lentils in a fine mesh strainer and place them in your iPot along with the water, brown sugar, can of diced tomatoes, BTB, tomato paste and spices. Put the cover on the iPot.

Hit the pressure cook button and set to 15 minutes on high pressure. While the Instant Pot® is doing it's thing, begin to dice and chop the red pepper, fresh tomatoes and celery.

Once the iPot is finished cooking, let it release pressure naturally for 10 minutes. Switch the handle to 'venting' and release the rest of the steam. Remove the lid.

Insert the remaining chopped veggies and corn in to the iPot. It should still be on the 'Keep Warm' setting. Put the lid back on and let it simmer for 10 minutes so the veggies soften up ever so slightly.

We love the crispiness of the veggies in this stew so that's why we don't cook them with the lentils. If you enjoy more of a mush, then just add them in at the start!

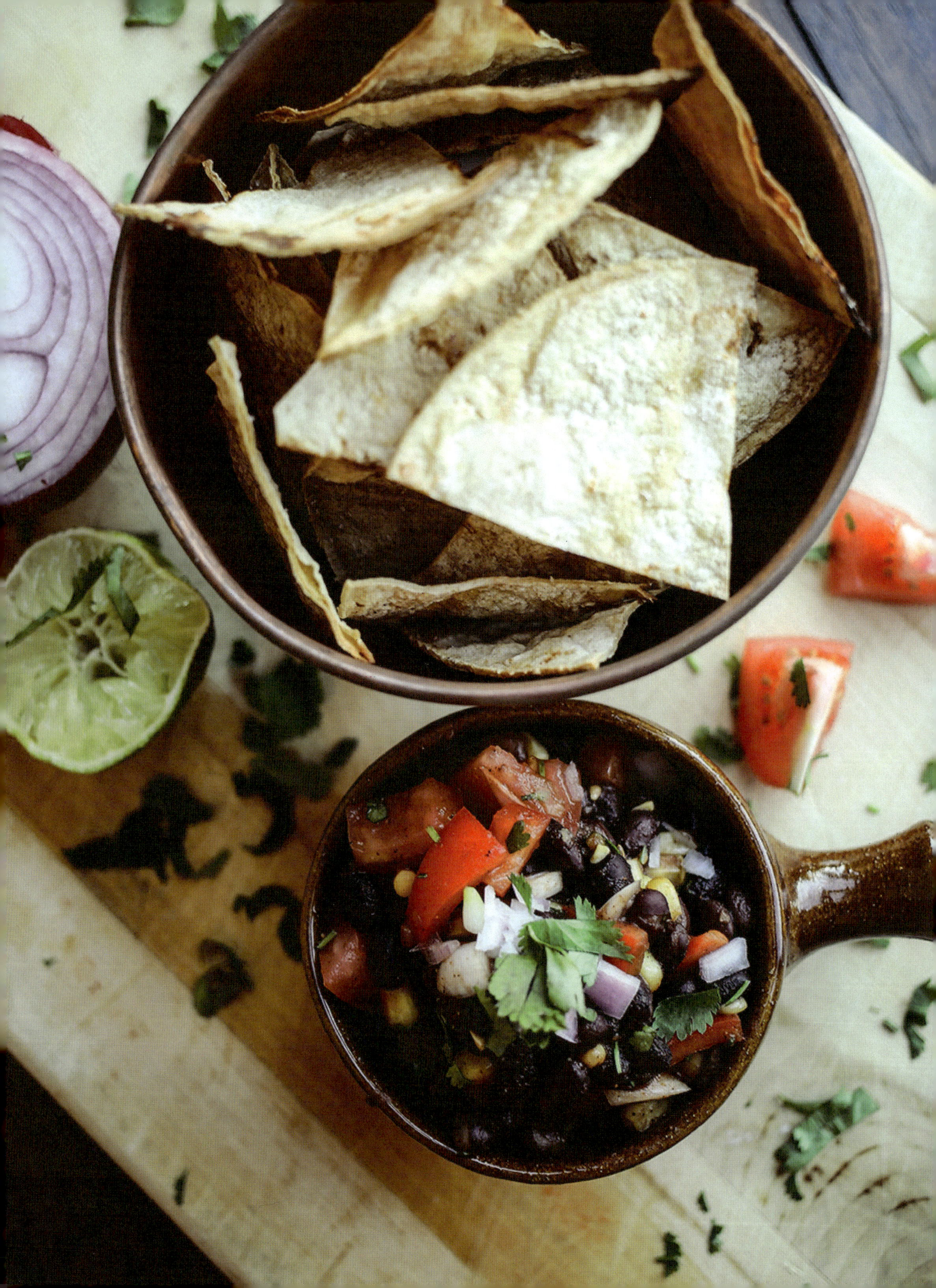

TEXAS COWBOY CAVIAR

Saddle up partner! Our own take on a classic cowboy caviar. We love all the fresh ingredients in this recipe. This is the type of recipe that tastes better the next day after it's marinated in the fridge over night. It goes great over fresh rice!

SERVINGS
3 x 170 calorie servings

PREP TIME
15 minutes

TOTAL COOK TIME
40 minutes

INGREDIENTS

CAVIAR
- 3/4 cup of dry black beans
- 1 1/2 cups of fresh or frozen corn
- 1 cup (1 medium tomato) of fresh tomatoes, diced
- 1/2 of a red pepper, chopped
- 1/4 cup of red onion, chopped
- 2 tbsp cilantro, chopped

SAUCE
- 1 can (7 3/4 oz or 220g) of mexican tomato sauce
- 1/2 tsp of salt
- 2 tsp of chili powder
- 2 tsp of brown sugar
- 1 tbsp of rice vinegar
- 1/2 of a lime squeezed

The brand of tomato sauce we used is 'El Pato' and can be found in the Mexican or Hispanic section of your grocery store. See the 'Ingredients We Use' chapter for more information.

METHOD

Rinse the beans in a strainer then place in iPot. Pour in about 3 cups of water and place the lid on.

Set the iPot on pressure cook for 25 minutes. Make sure the handle is set to 'sealing'. You can prepare the tomatoes, red pepper, onion and cilantro during this time. When the beans are done cooking, hit the 'Cancel' button and allow the pressure to come down naturally for 10 minutes on high pressure. Release the remaining steam using the release valve.

Mix all of the sauce ingredients together in to a small bowl. Drain the beans in to a strainer and place them in to a bowl or a container you'll be storing them in. Place the remaining caviar ingredients in there as well and pour the sauce ingredients over the bowl of caviar ingredients. Stir to get an even coating.

✳✳✳
D's Epic Tip

To make oil-free corn chips, take some corn tortillas and slice them. Bake them at 400F for 8 - 10 minutes with lime juice and salt on top.

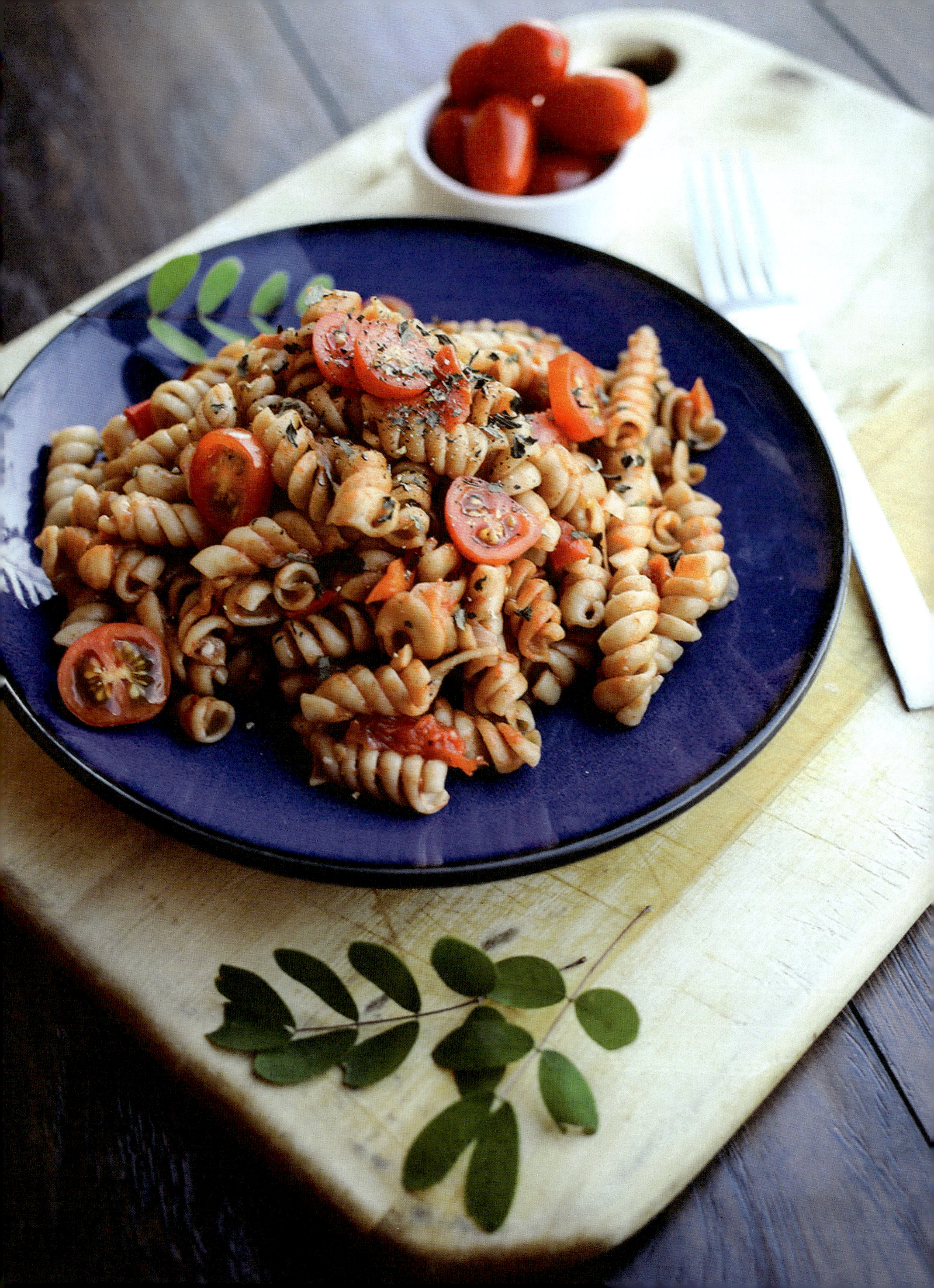

ONE POT PASTA BRAH!

We really weren't sure how this one pot pasta would turn out but boy oh boy were we impressed! If you were wondering if you could do pasta in the Instant Pot®... well you can check that one off your list cause this is the bomb dizzle!

SERVINGS	PREP TIME	TOTAL COOK TIME
3 x 600 calorie servings	10 minutes	25 minutes

INGREDIENTS

PASTA

1/2	of a yellow onion, diced
1	red pepper, chopped
3	cloves of garlic, minced
1/4	cup of fresh basil, chopped
1	lb (454g) of rotini noodles
1/2	of a can of tomato paste
1	lb (454g) of tomatoes, chopped
3 3/4	cups (30 oz) of water
2	tbsp of sriracha (optional)

GARNISH

Fresh basil

Black pepper

METHOD

Chop up the onion, red pepper, garlic and basil. Add about 1/4 cup of water in to the Instant Pot® and hit the sautée button. Add in the onion, red pepper, garlic and basil. Sautée for about 5 minutes stirring frequently to avoid any burning.

While it is sautéing, chop up your tomatoes and add them in to the Instant Pot® when the 5 minutes is up. Add in the water, tomato paste and noodles. Stir everything very well.

Put the top on and make sure the steam release handle is set to 'sealing'. Hit the pressure cook button and set to 8 minutes on high pressure. If you want it 'al dente', set it to 6 minutes.

When the time is up, release the steam immediately. Remove the lid and serve with extra basil and black pepper on top.

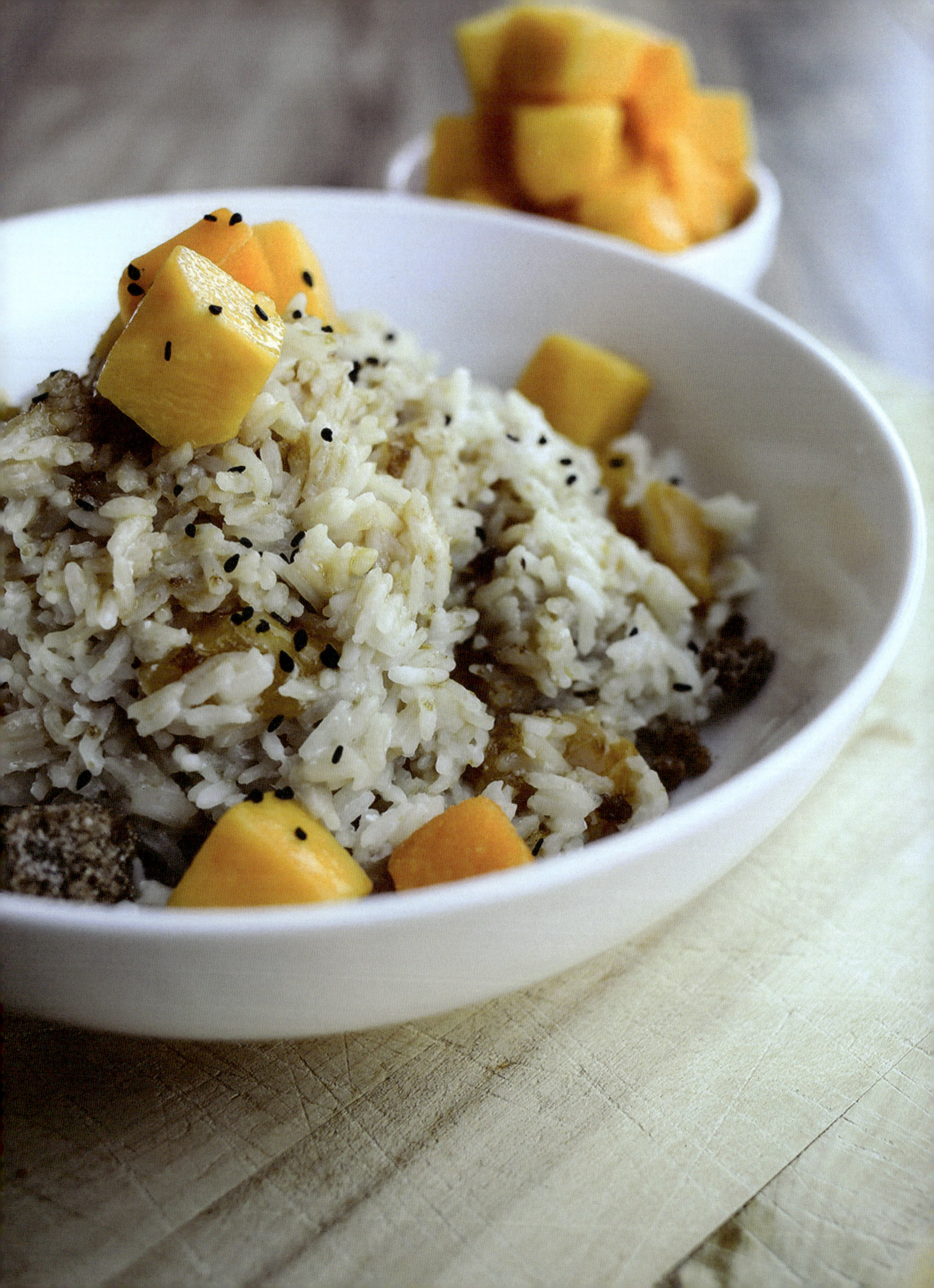

MANGO STICKY RICE

Memories of SE Asia anyone? Mango sticky rice is a nice delectable breakfast that is rich, creamy and sweet. Can you do it in the Instant Pot®? Ya damn right you can!

SERVINGS	PREP TIME	TOTAL COOK TIME
2 x 500 calorie servings	5 minutes	20 minutes

INGREDIENTS

- 1 cup of white jasmine rice
- 1 1/4 cups (+ 1/3 cup) of light sweetened coconut milk
- 1 cup of frozen mango chunks
- 2 tbsp of brown sugar

GARNISH
Black sesame seeds (optional)

*** D's Epic Tip
Periodically check your condensation collector on the back of your Instant Pot®. If it fills up all the way, it will fill the sealing rim area and prevent the iPot from sealing properly

METHOD

Measure out 1 cup of white jasmine rice and 1 1/4 cups of light coconut milk and place in to your Instant Pot®.

We used Trader Joe's vanilla coconut milk which comes in the cardboard tetra pack. It isn't the normal coconut milk that comes in a can. If you found a light coconut milk in a tin that could work or you could also use non-dairy milk like almond or soy. We just like the coconut milk, it smells almost like rice krispee squares when it's finished cooking.

Place the mango chunks on top of the rice and coconut milk and set the iPot on pressure cook for 4 minutes on high pressure. Make sure the steam release handle is set to 'sealing' and put the lid on top.

When the timer is up, let the iPot naturally release until the float valve drops. This should take 10-15 minutes.

Mix in some extra coconut milk in to the iPot and mix it around (about 1/3 cup). Spoon the rice and mango mixture in to a serving bowl and sprinkle the brown sugar and seasame seeds on top. Enjoy!

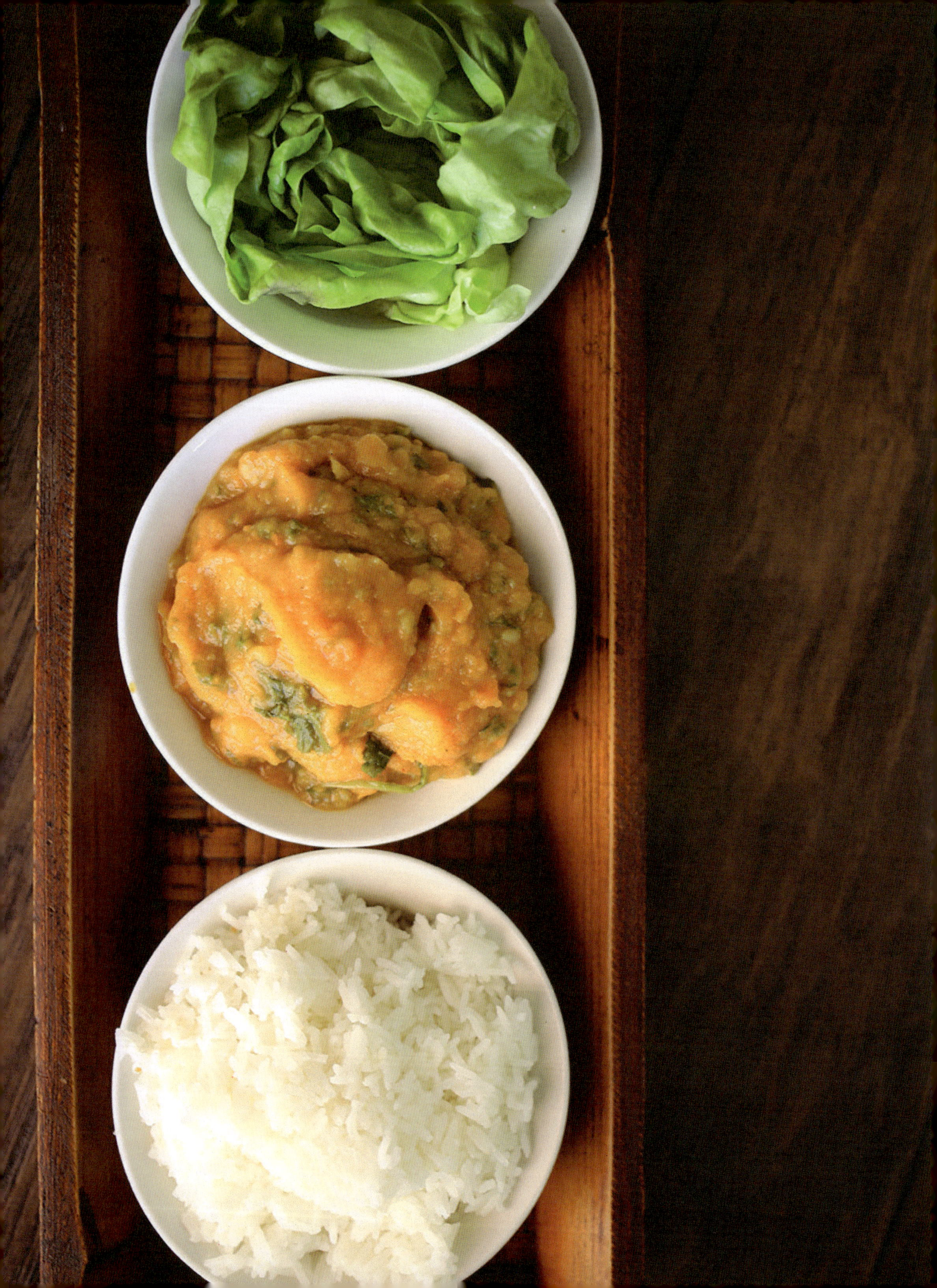

CARROT POTATO SOUP

Remember the times when your mother would make you carrot soup? Maybe? No?? Well... We do and it was freaking delicious. hope this soup reminds you of those times.

SERVINGS	PREP TIME	TOTAL COOK TIME
2 x 350 calorie servings	15 minutes	25 minutes

INGREDIENTS

- 5 medium potatoes, peeled and chopped
- 8 carrots, peeled and chopped
- 1/2 of a yellow onion, chopped
- 1/4 cup powdered peanut butter
- 3 cloves of garlic, minced
- 2 cups of frozen (or fresh) kale, finely chopped
- 1 tbsp of curry powder
- 1 tsp of cayenne pepper
- 4 cups of water
- 2 tsp of Better Than Bouillon (if you don't use the BTB, substitute 2 cups of water with 2 cups of veggie broth)

METHOD

Ok, here's what you want to do first. Mince the garlic and chop the onion. Place those in your Instant Pot® with about 1/4 cup of water and hit the 'Sautée' button. Let the onions and garlic sautée for about 5 minutes.

Add in the Better Than Bouillon, powdered peanut butter, curry powder and cayenne. Mix it around and if you need to add a bit more water then you can. Let this sautée for another 2 minutes.

Add in the remaining ingredients (except for the kale), put the lid on and set the Instant Pot® to pressure cook for 8 minutes on high pressure.

Once the time is up, let it naturally release for 10-15 minutes. Switch the steam release handle to 'venting' to release any extra steam. Remove the lid.

Use an immersion blender and give the soup short zaps until you get the desired consistency. If you don't have an immersion blender, take half of the soup blend it and mix it back in with the soup.

Add in the chopped frozen kale and mix once again.

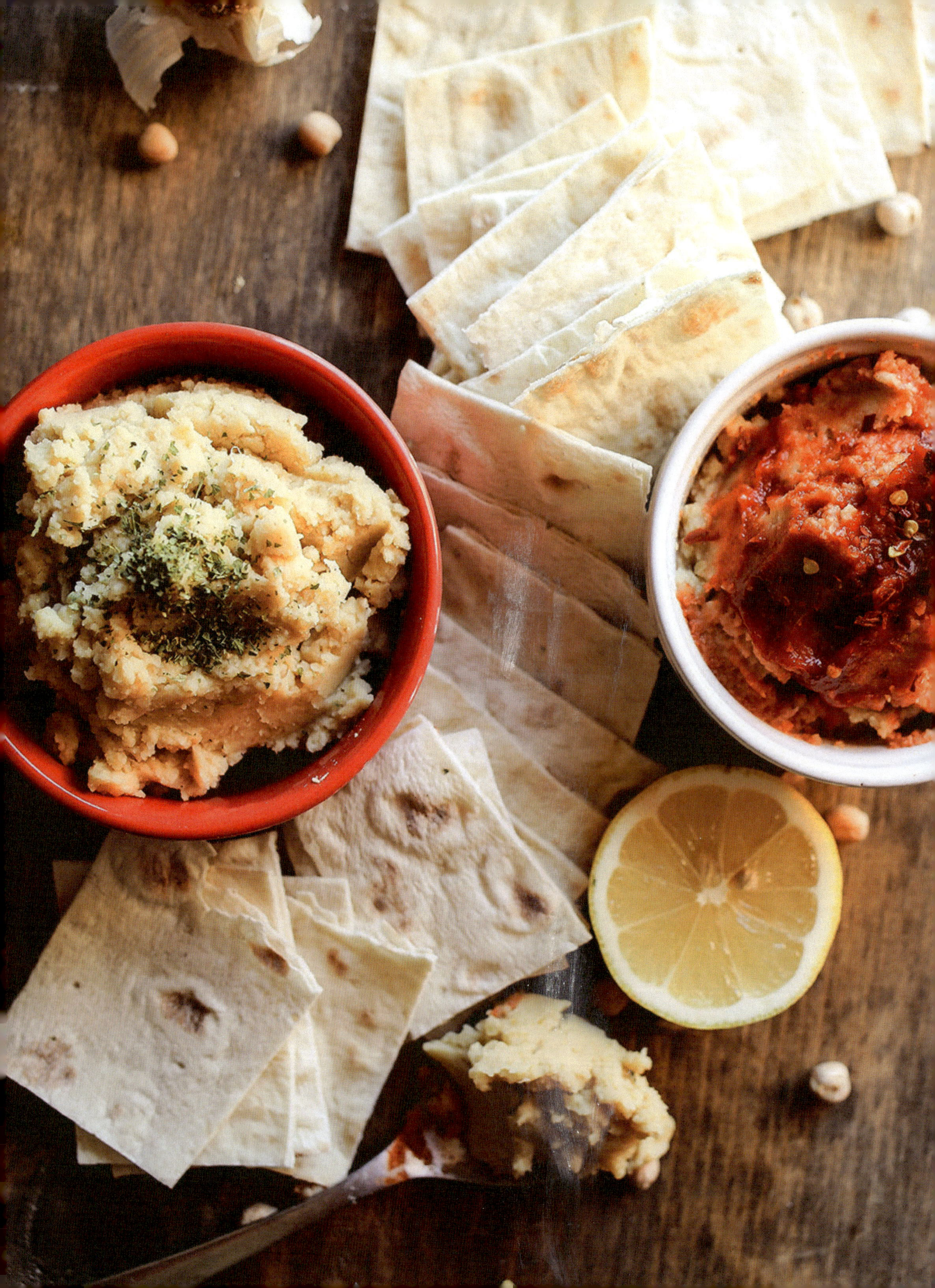

HUMDINGER HUMMUS

Finding a healthy hummus can be really tricky! Don't worry, using your Instant Pot® you can make a healthy hummus from scratch. We put hummus all over everything. Ya... you heard us... everything. Chilis, Stews, Rice, Crackers... everything.

SERVINGS	PREP TIME	TOTAL COOK TIME
2 x 500 calorie servings	5 minutes	70 minutes

INGREDIENTS

1	cup of dry garbanzo beans
2	cups of water
2	garlic cloves
1/2	tsp of salt
1	tsp of cumin
1/2	lemon, juice of

METHOD

First thing you want to do is rinse your dry garbanzo beans really well. A clean garbanzo bean is a happy garbanzo bean.

Combine the beans and water in the Instant Pot® and cook for 60 minutes on the pressure cook setting, high pressure. Don't forget to move the steam release handle to 'sealing'. Hannah has forgotten too many times and always blames Dewie.

When the time is up, use the quick release method to release the steam immediately. We cook the garbanzo beans a little bit longer than is recommened to make sure they are nice and soft.

Place the garbanzo beans in a high speed blender along with the remaining ingredients. Make sure you pour in the water that was left over after cooking the beans, don't throw it down the drain!

Blend that lovely mixture on high until creamy smooth. Enjoy!

✳✳✳
D's Epic Tip

When using dry beans which we use a lot of in this book, make sure to rinse and sort through the beans for any pebbles or small rocks. Chomping down on one of these could be very painful and send you to the dentist! Ouchies!

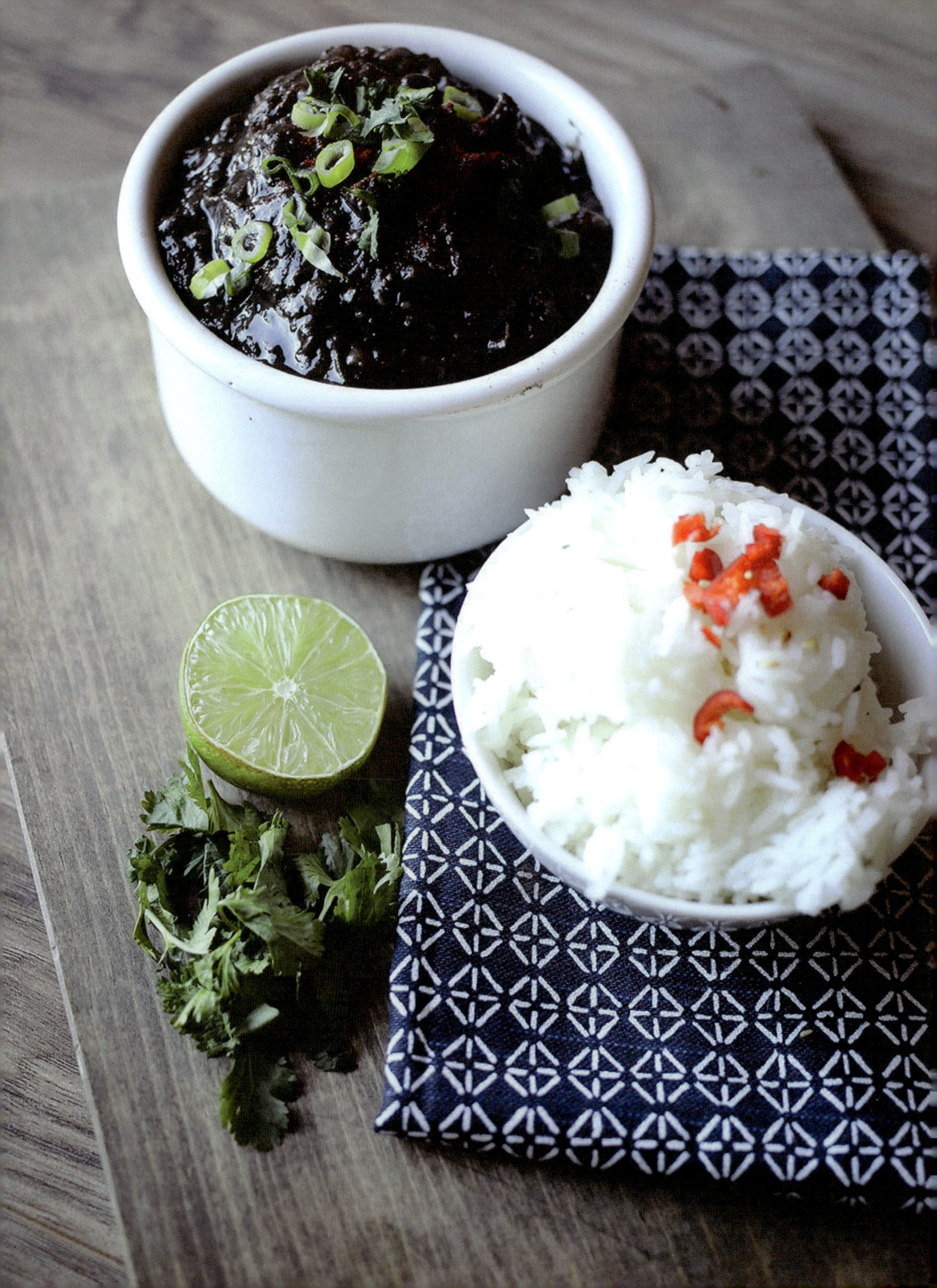

BLACK BEAN SOUP OF GLORY

Hannah is so obsessed with black bean soup. Right from the get go of making this recipe book, she was obsessing over this recipe. So here you go, a delicious black bean soup. We love this as a delicious topping over rice or steamed potatoes.

SERVINGS
2 x 500 calorie servings

PREP TIME
10 minutes

TOTAL COOK TIME
60 minutes

INGREDIENTS

- 3 cups dry black beans, rinsed
- 1 large yellow onion, diced
- 1 carrot, chopped
- 3 stalks of celery, minced
- 6 garlic cloves, minced
- 4 1/2 cups of water
- 2 tsp Better Than Bouillon (if you don't have BTB then subsitute 2 cups of water for 2 cups of veggie broth)
- 1 tbsp of cumin
- 1 tsp of chili powder
- 1 tsp of cayenne pepper
- 1 lime, juice of
- 1/4 cup of cilantro

METHOD

Make sure to rinse and sort through your dried beans very well. Sometimes small rocks or pebbles can be found in the beans and could end up in your food which may result in a trip to the dentist.

Add all of the ingredients (except the lime juice and cilantro) in to the Instant Pot® and give it a jolly good stir. Make sure the vent on top is set to 'sealing' and put the lid on. Set the cooker on pressure cook for 30 minutes on high pressure.

Once finished, let the steam release nautrally. That should take about 15-20 minutes or so. The silver release valve should have dropped but if it hasn't, switch the steam release handle to 'venting' to release any extra steam.

Add in the lime juice and cilantro. Lightly blend the soup using an immersion blender. If you don't have an immersion blender, take about 1/2 or 3/4 of the soup and blend in a blender. Mix the soup back together.

Optionally you can add some avocado, tortilla chips or salsa to accompany this bomb diggity black bean soup!

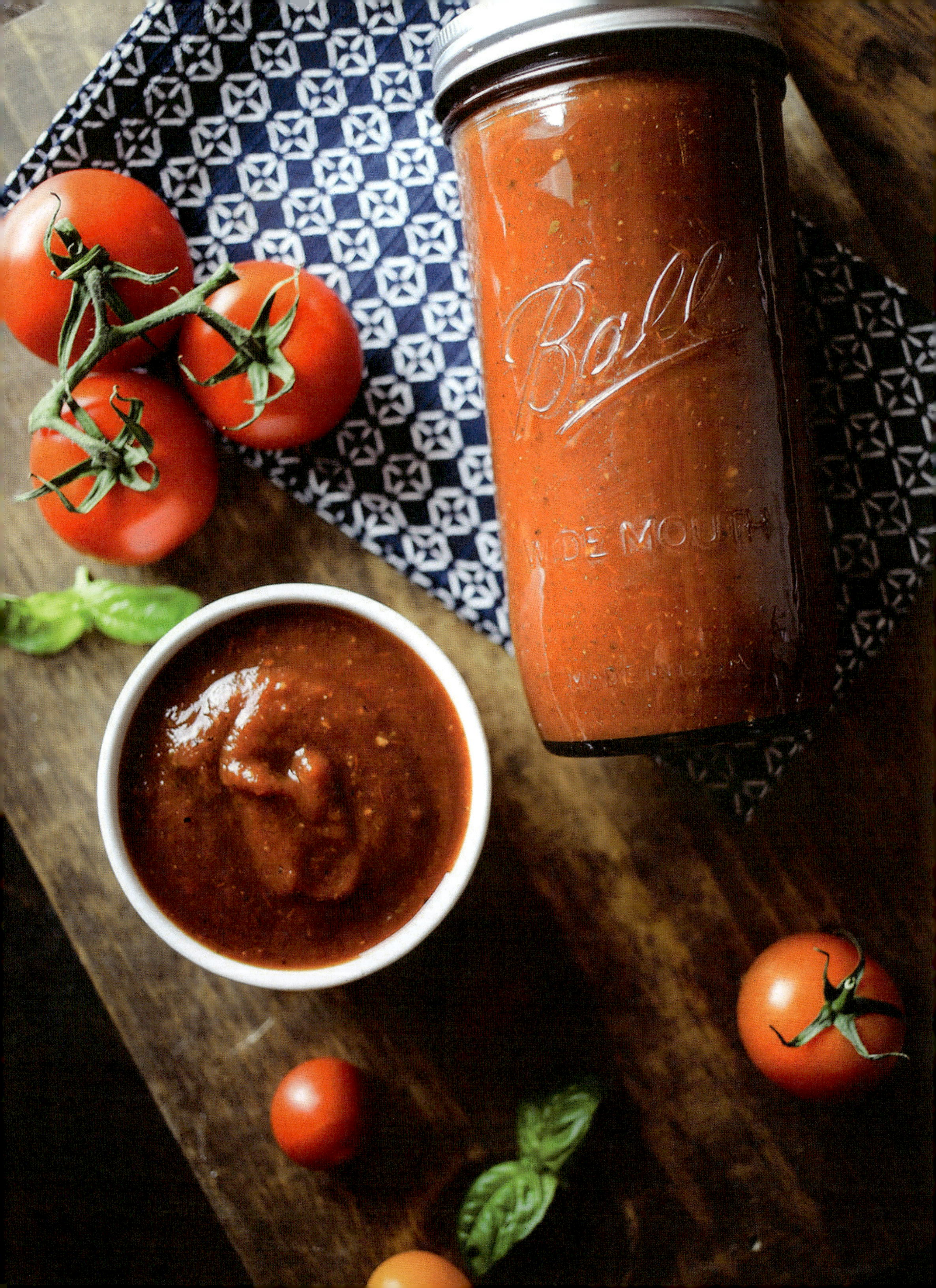
Ball
WIDE MOUTH

NO OIL MARINARA SAUCE

Man oh man it can be difficult to find a marinara sauce that doesn't have any oil in it. We've got you covered though. You can make this and use it with the one pot pasta recipe!

SERVINGS	PREP TIME	TOTAL COOK TIME
Makes 4 - 6 cups	10 minutes	45 minutes

INGREDIENTS

- 2 lbs (910g) of tomatoes, diced
- 2 cans of tomato paste
- 3 cups of water
- 1 red onion, chopped
- 1 red pepper, chopped
- 2 tsp of salt
- 1/4 cup of brown sugar
- 2 tbsp of Italian seasoning
- 6 cloves of garlic, minced
- 1/2 cup basil, chopped

METHOD

Mince the garlic and chop the onion. Place those in to the Instant Pot®. Add in 1/2 cup of water and hit the sautée button. Use a wooden spoon or spatula to stir the onions and garlic while it sautées for 5 minutes.

Remove the inner pot from the iPot and add in the rest of your ingredients except for the basil. Put the pot back in the iPot and put the lid on. Set the Instant Pot® to pressure cook for 15 minutes on high pressure and make sure the steam release handle is set to 'sealing'.

Once the time is up, move the steam release handle to 'venting'. Remove the lid and place the chopped basil in the pot. Then take an immersion blender and blend the sauce right in the Instant Pot® until it is smooth.

Hit the sautée button and let it boil for 10 minutes or until it reaches the desired consistency. Hit the 'Cancel' button let the sauce cool down a bit and place air tight mason jars. Store in the fridge for up to 2 weeks. Before using, just check and make sure the sauce is still fresh.

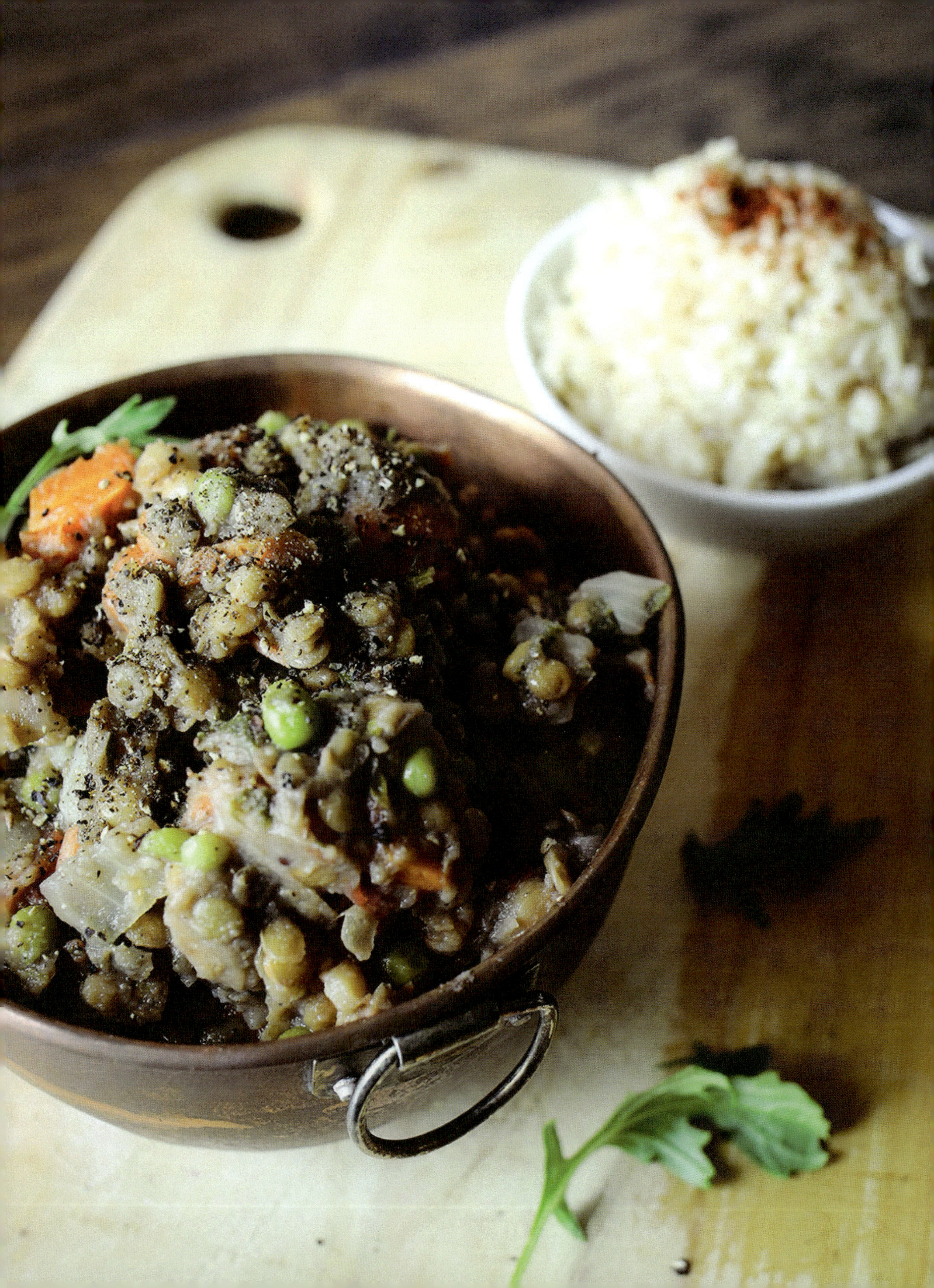

VEGGIE LENTIL SOUP A LOOOP

Need a delicious warm filling soup? This is the one for you then! Chopped full of delicious vegetables this is a great soup for those cooler nights of the year.

SERVINGS
3 x 500 calorie servings

PREP TIME
10 minutes

TOTAL COOK TIME
30 minutes

INGREDIENTS

- 1 cup of green lentils
- 5 medium potatoes, chopped
- 1 yellow onion, chopped
- 2 or 3 ribs of celery, chopped
- 2 carrots, chopped
- 2 bay leaves
- 1 cup of green peas (canned or frozen)
- 1 can (14.5 fl oz or 429mL) of diced tomoatoes
- 1 cup of spinach or kale, finely chopped (fresh or frozen)
- 3 1/2 cups of water
- 3 cloves of garlic, minced
- 2 tsp of black pepper
- 2 tsp of better than boullion (if you don't have BTB then subsitute 2 cups of water for 2 cups of veggie broth)

METHOD

Prepare and chop the potatoes, onion, celery, carrots and mince the garlic.

Add all the prepared ingredients to the Instant Pot® a long with any remaining ingredients except for the green peas and spinach or kale.

Put the lid on and set the iPot to 10 minutes on pressure cook, high pressure. Once it is finished cooking. Let the steam naturally release for about 15 or 20 minutes. When that time is up, release the remaining steam using the steam release handle. Remove the lid.

Add in the green peas and spinach or kale. Stir everything around really well. Let the Instant Pot® stay in the 'Keep Warm' mode for about 10 minutes while the frozen peas dethaw (if you used frozen ones).

Your veggie soup a loop is ready to serve! Make sure to remove the bay leaves when you spot them. When serving, add some salt or pepper to taste.

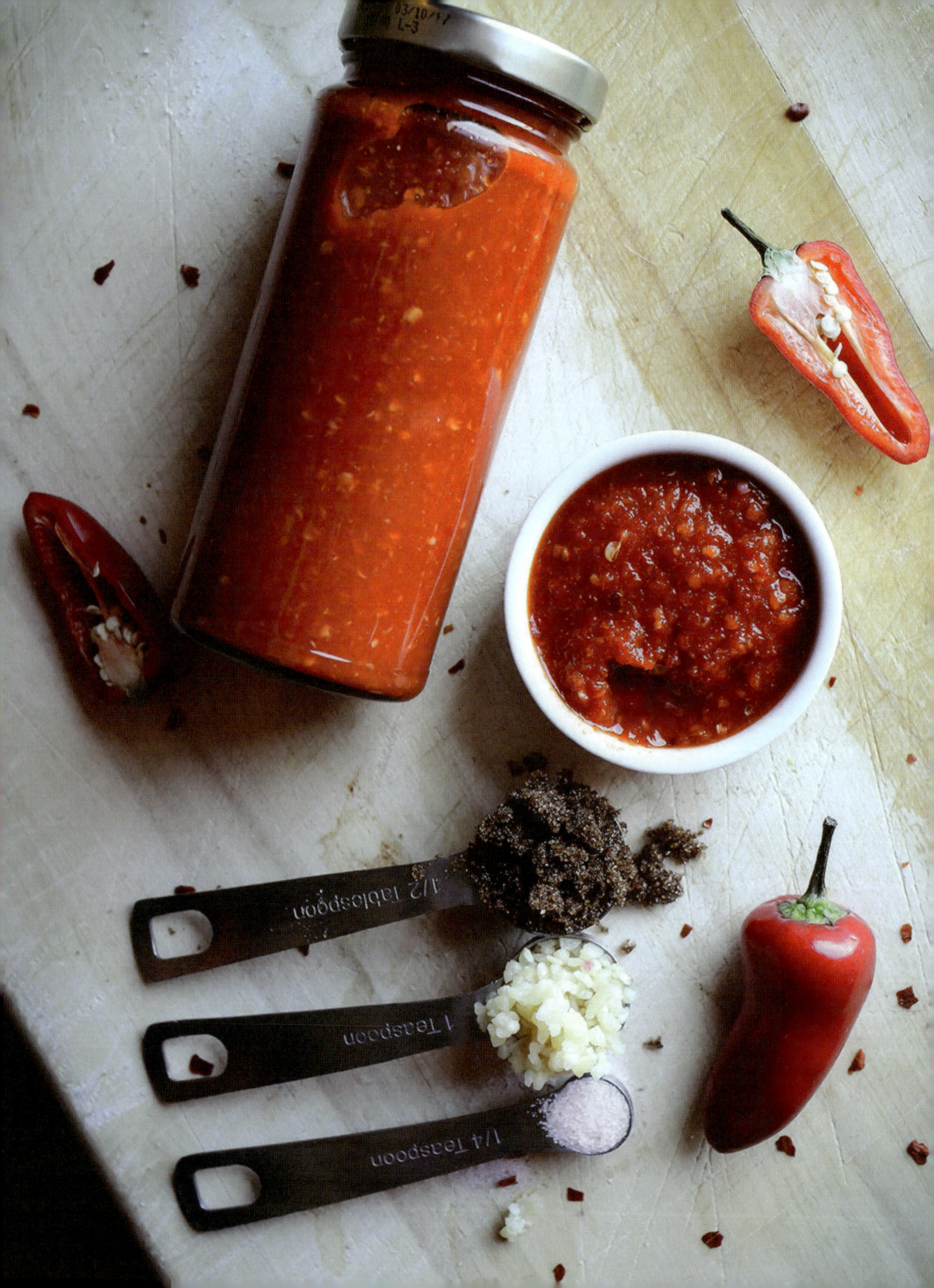
1/2 Tablespoon
1 Teaspoon
1/4 Teaspoon

IT'S COMING OUT HOT SRIRACHA

This isn't your typical Instant Pot® recipe. We wanted to show you that this device is versatile. The sautée setting can boil down sauces. You can make all types of sauces at home that are free of preservatives and ingredients you want to stay away from.

SERVINGS	PREP TIME	TOTAL COOK TIME
Makes around 2 cups	5 minutes	25 minutes

INGREDIENTS

- 1   lb of hot red chili peppers (fresno, jalapeno, etc.)
- 3   tbsp of brown sugar
- 6   garlic cloves, peeled
- 1/2 cup of distilled vinegar
- 1   tbsp of salt
- 1/3 cup of water

** If you can't find hot red peppers, you can always use hot green peppers like serrano or jalapeno, it just means you'll have a green sriracha instead of red.

METHOD

You want to take all of your chili peppers and chop of all of them stems and put them directly in to your blender.

Add the remaining ingredients to the blender and blend on high until everything is liquified. Some of the seeds may still be intact which is fine.

Pour the sriracha mixture in to the iPot. Hit the sautée button. Then hit the 'Adjust' button twice to move the heat setting to 'Less'.

Let the sriracha mixture sautée for 15 minutes stirring on occasion. Once the 15 minutes is up, let the sauce cool for 10-15 minutes.

We store our sriracha in old glass sauce containers. It should last at least 2 weeks if you keep it in the fridge.

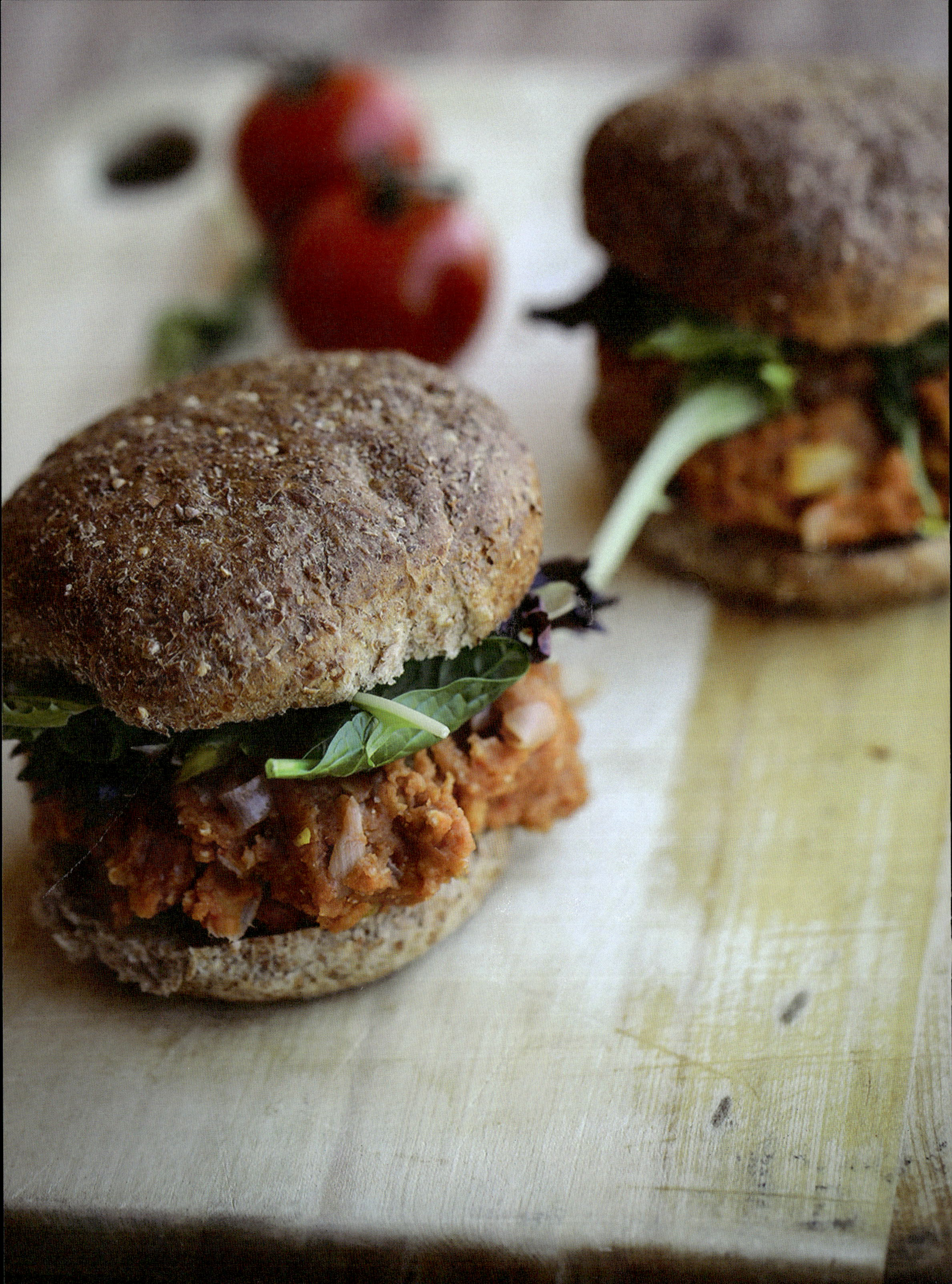

THE SLOPPIEST JOE (YOU'LL EVER KNOW)

We hope you like your Joe's extra sloppy! Extra Sloppy!!
We can hear you now, "Woh... wohh.. you're creeping us out Derek & Hannah!!
Bonus points to you if you know what movie we're referencing.

SERVINGS	PREP TIME	TOTAL COOK TIME
Enough for 6-8 sloppy joes	10 minutes	25 minutes

INGREDIENTS

- 1 cup of red lentils
- 1 yellow onion, chopped
- 1 rib of celery, chopped
- 1/2 of a yellow pepper, chopped
- 1/2 can (1/2 of a 8 oz can) of tomato paste
- 2 tbsp of brown sugar
- 2 1/2 cups of water
- 1/4 cup of red wine vinegar
- 1 tsp of liquid smoke
- 1 tsp of salt
- 3 garlic cloves, minced
- 1/4 cup of oil-free bread crumbs
- 2 tbsp of sriracha (optional)

6 or 8 oil-free hamburger buns**

** In the picture we used Ezekiel 4:9 Sprouted Whole Grain Burger Buns that we found at our local store. Stores like Whole Foods or Sprouts should have them. Be sure to check the freezer section because they are usually in there.

METHOD

This is a pretty easy recipe but it creates an awesome dish that you could serve any family or friend.

Combine all the ingredients, except the bread crumbs, in to the Instant Pot®. Make sure the steam release handle is set to 'sealing' and hit the pressure cook button. Put the lid on and set for 15 minutes on high pressure.

Let the pressure release naturally for 10-15 minutes. Move the steam release handle to 'venting' to release any extra steam. Remove the lid. Add in the bread crumbs and stir.

Serve the sloppy Joe mix on hamburger buns and top with some fresh mixed greens if you're feeling it. Maybe you're not. Who knows. We also love the Joes with sliced yellow banana peppers for a spicy crunch.

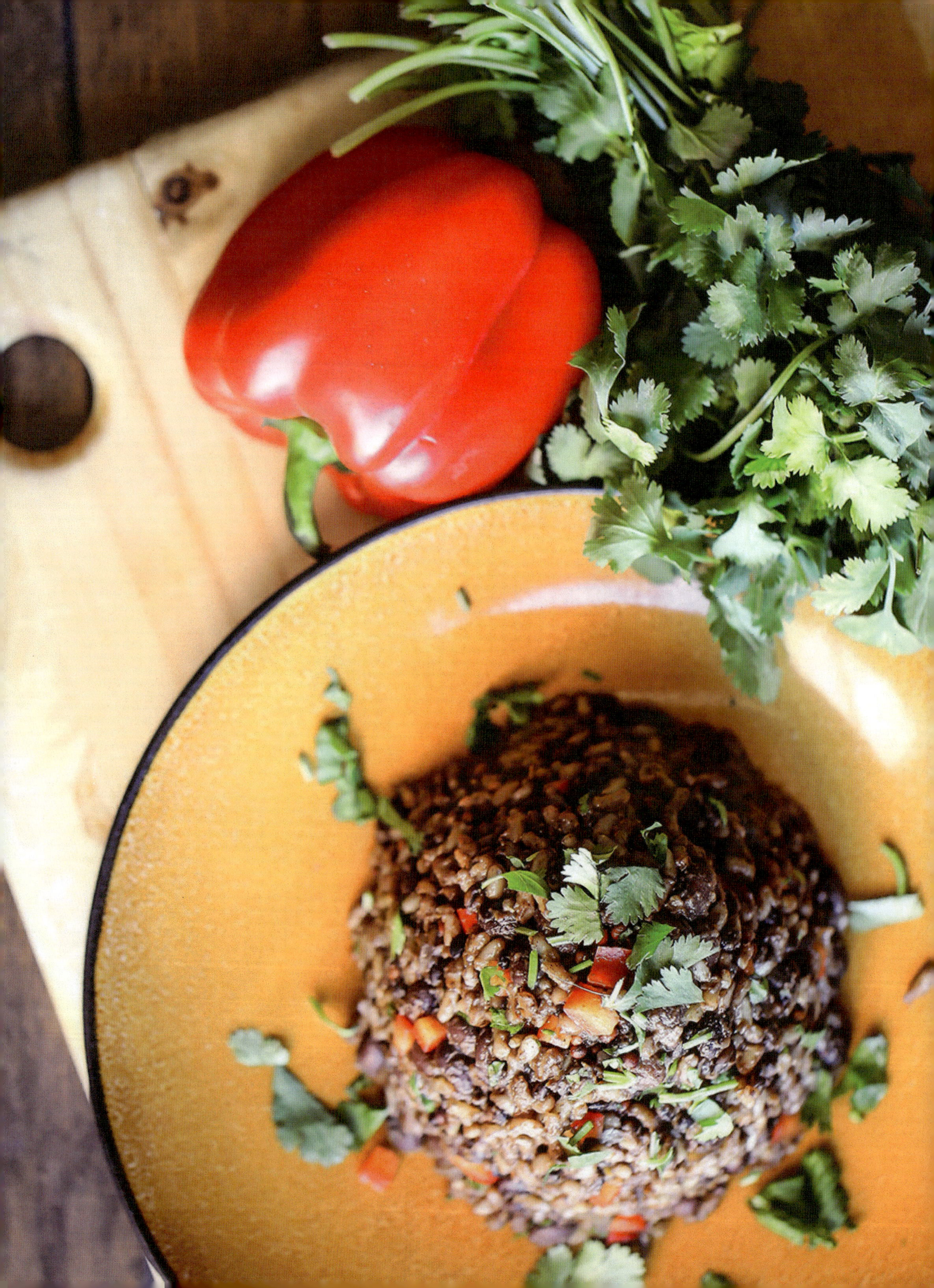

BOMB DIGGITY BLACK BEAN RICE

Rice and beans is a staple for so many people on a plant-based diet. This dish is de… and cooks the brown rice and dried black beans perfectly. They have almost the s… cooking time in the Ipot so it works perfectly together. Enjoy!

SERVINGS	PREP TIME	TOTAL COOK TIME
2 x 500 calorie servings	10 minutes	45 minutes

INGREDIENTS

- 1 cup brown rice medley (just use regular brown rice if you don't have a brown rice medley)
- 1/2 cup of dry black beans
- 2 1/2 cups of water
- 1/2 red onion, diced
- 1/2 red pepper, diced
- 2 garlic cloves, minced
- 1 tsp Better Than Bouillon or a bouillon cube
- 1 tbsp chili powder
- 1/2 tsp cayenne pepper
- 1 tsp cumin

METHOD

First thing you want to do is mince the garlic and dice the onion. Add them in to the Instant Pot along with 1/2 cup of water and hit the 'Sautée' button. Let it sautée for 5 minutes. Hit the 'Cancel' button.

Add in the remaining ingredients in to the Instant Pot (except for the red pepper). Put the cover on the iPot and set the steam release handle to 'sealing'. Put the lid on top. Hit the pressure cook button and set the time to 25 minutes on high pressure.

Once finished cooking, let the iPot naturally release for 10-15 minutes. Switch the steam release handle to 'venting' to release the remaining steam. Remove the lid.

Add in the diced red pepper and now you are ready to enjoy this delicious meal!

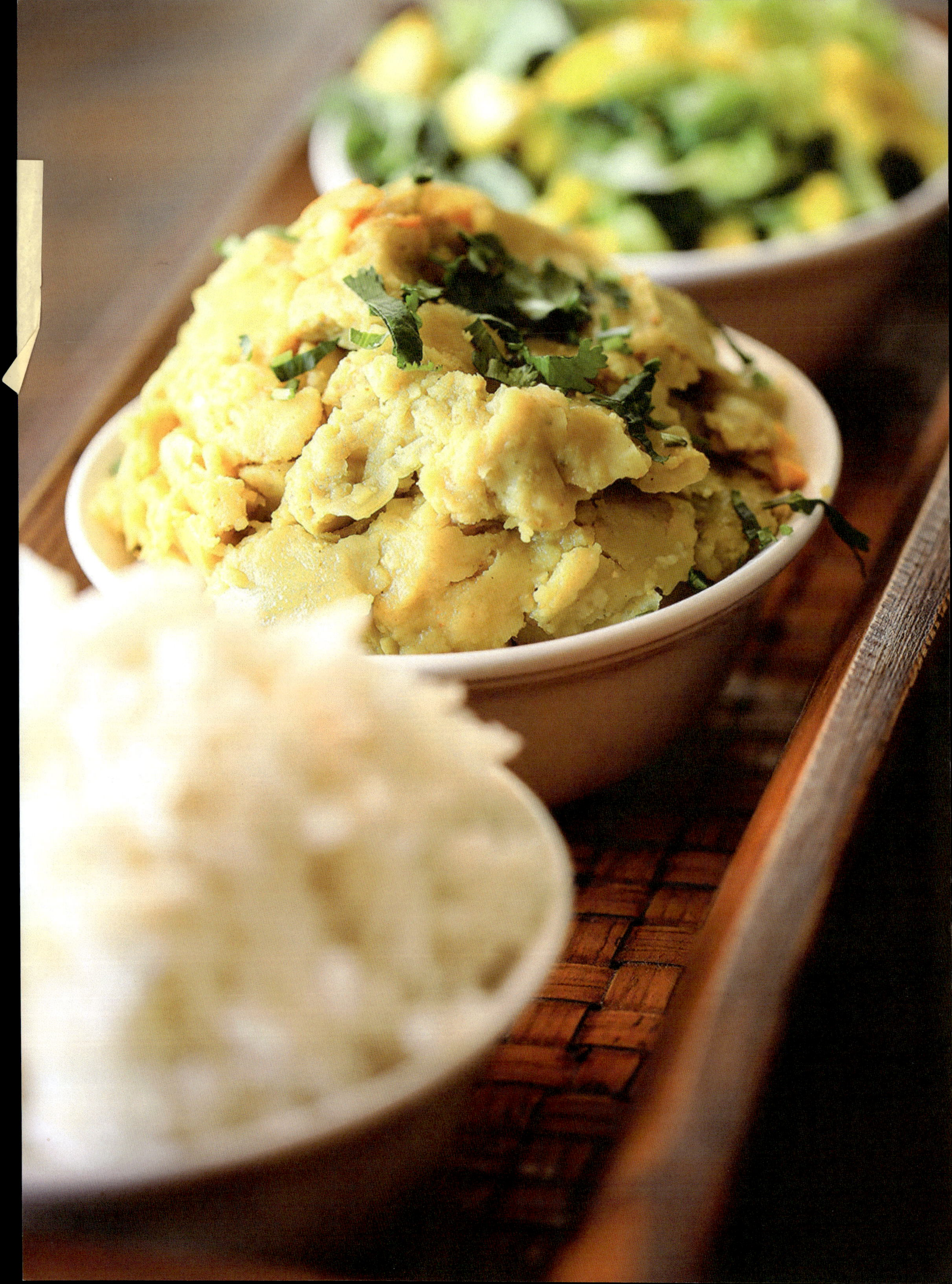

DAL, DHAL OR DAHL?

We didn't know what the proper name or spelling for this recipe would be. We contacted our advisors and they said that in order to not annoy anyone, we should just call it all 3. There ya go!

SERVINGS	PREP TIME	TOTAL COOK TIME
3 x 450 calorie servings	5 minutes	30 minutes

INGREDIENTS

- 2 cups of red lentils
- 6 cups of water
- 1 orange (or yellow) bell pepper, chopped
- 1 yellow onion, chopped
- 3 garlic cloves, minced
- 1/2 lemon, juice of
- 1 tsp of turmeric
- 1 tsp of curry powder
- 1 tsp of cumin
- 1 tsp of fresh ginger, minced
- 1/4 tsp of cayenne pepper

METHOD

Ok here we go. This dal, dhal or dahl is super delicious. Like most things we make, it's great with rice. Brown or white... we don't discriminate.

Combine all of your ingredients in to your Instant Pot®. Place the lid on and set the iPot to 15 minutes on pressure cook, high pressure. Make sure the steam release handle is set to 'sealing'.

When it is finished cooking, let it naturally release for 10-15 minutes. Turn the steam release handle to 'venting' to release the last bit of steam.

It's all ready to eat!

✱✱✱
D's Epic Tip

At this point in the book you might be thinking to yourself, wow you guys use lentils a lot. ya... we do. They're delicious. this isn't really a tip, more of an observational statement. whatever.

HIGHCARBHANNAH.CO | EPIC VEGAN PRESSURE COOKING

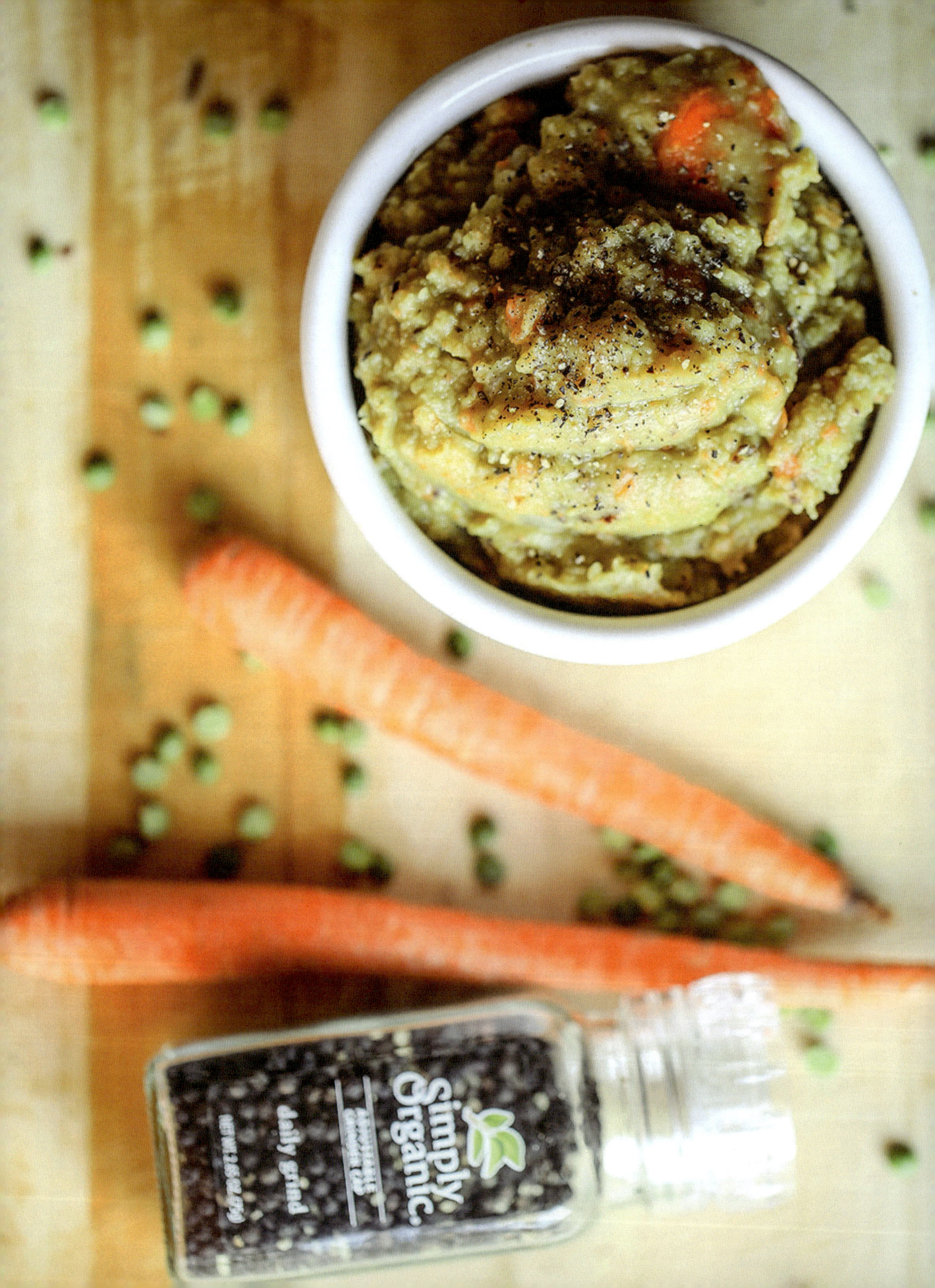
Simply Organic.
daily grind

SPLIT 'EM UP PEA SOUP

soups are just so easy to do in the Instant Pot®. cooking at pressure speeds up the cooking time so much. less time waiting for food to finish and more time watching netflix. Cause what else are you going to do with all that extra time? Save the planet???

SERVINGS	PREP TIME	TOTAL COOK TIME
3 x 480 calorie servings	10 minutes	25 minutes

INGREDIENTS

- 2 cups of green split peas
- 3-4 medium sized carrots, chopped
- 4 cups of water
- 1/2 of a large yellow onion, chopped
- 1/2 tsp of ground black pepper
- 2 garlic cloves, minced
- 1 tbsp of veggie better than bouillon or 1 veggie bouillon cube (you could also sub 3 cups of water for 3 cups of veggie broth)

*** D's Epic Tip

Better than Bouillon and most bouillon cubes will have oil in them. Most Vegetable broths do not. If you are going 100% strict no oil then go for the broth but we think the amount of oil in the BTB or Cubes is pretty trivial.

METHOD

Chop up the onion and mince the garlic. Throw those in to the Instant Pot® along with 1/3 cup of water and hit the sautée button. Let it sautée for about 5-7 minutes until the onions become translucent.

Combine the remaining ingredients (except the black pepper) in to the Instant Pot®. Place the lid on and set it to 7 minutes on pressure cook, high pressure. This soup is a quickie in the iPot. Make sure the steam release handle is set to 'sealing'.

When the time is complete, let the iPot naturally release for 15 minutes. You may want to let it cool down for a few minutes. Add in your black pepper use your immersion blender to blend the soup. Use short zaps so that you still leave some chunks. If you don't have an immersion blender, ladle 3/4 of the soup in to a blender then reintroduce once blended with the rest of the soup.

Enjoy!

If the soup is too thick, try adding in a bit more water. Remember that it thickens up when it cools down!

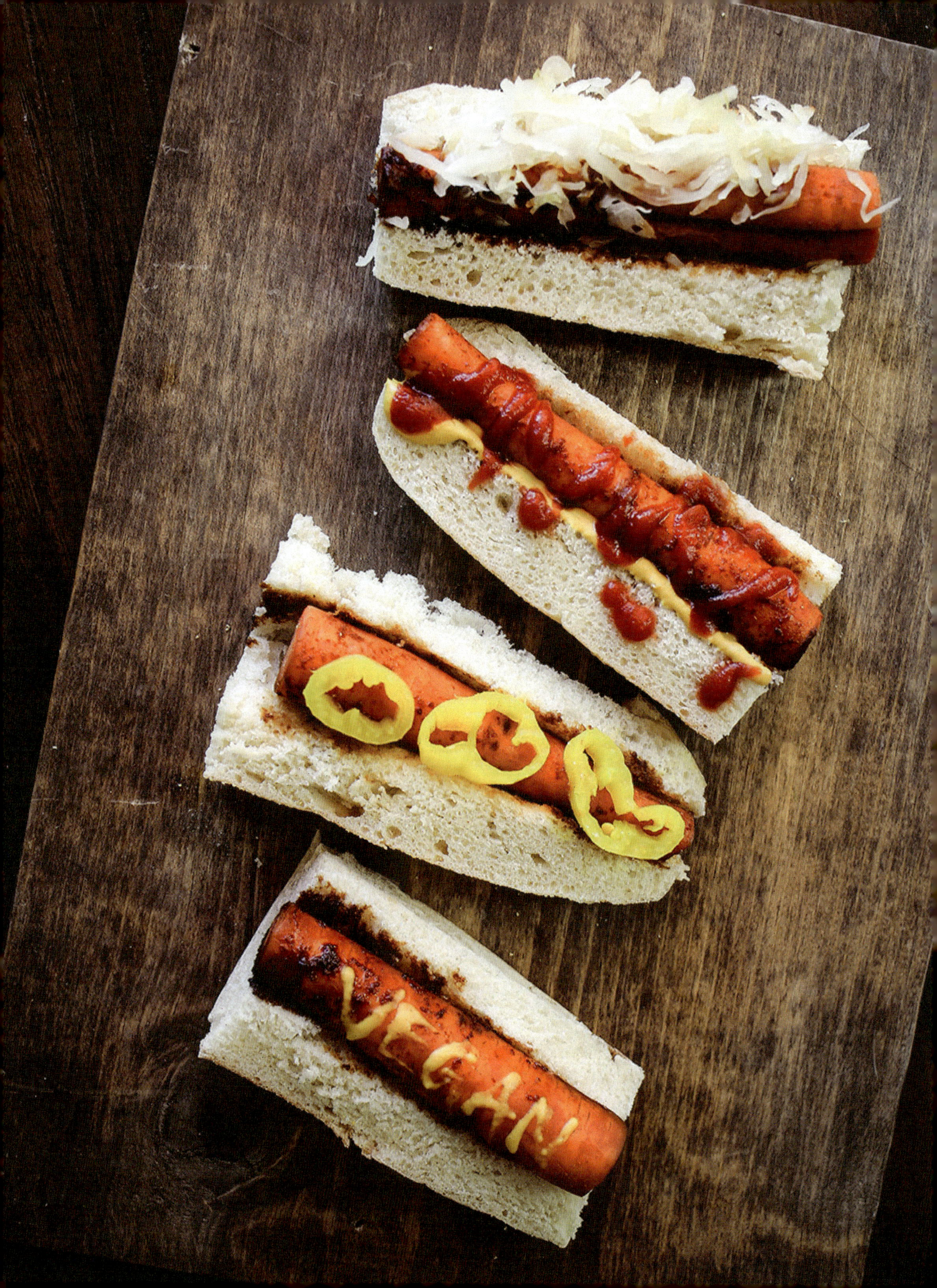
VEGAN

NACHO MOM'S HOT DOGS

We know what you're thinking... hot dogs?? In the Instant Pot®?? Oh yes! And what does your mom have to do with it? No idea, it was a funny recipe name. Enjoy this very different ipot recipe!

SERVINGS	PREP TIME	TOTAL COOK TIME
Makes 4 hot dogs	15 minutes	20 minutes

INGREDIENTS

MARINADE INGREDIENTS

- 1/4 cup of soy sauce
- 1/4 cup of water
- 1 tbsp of rice vinegar
- 1/2 tsp of liquid smoke
- 1/2 tsp of garlic powder
- 1/2 tsp of onion powder

TOPPINGS
Ketchup, mustard, etc

HOT DOG INGREDIENTS

- 4 large carrots
- 4 oil-free vegan hot dog buns **

** Finding oil-free hot dog buns could prove difficult for you. In the photo we took a half-baked bread loaf from Trader Joe's and sliced it to resemble hot dog buns. Search for Ezekiel 4:9 hot dog buns or use any vegan oil-free buns or rolls you can find.

METHOD

Place the trivet (the metal rack thing that came with your Instant Pot®) in the inner pot. Pour in 1 1/2 cups of water. Place your 4 carrots on the trivet and put the lid on. Set the iPot to pressure cook for 3 minutes on high pressure. Make sure the steam release handle is set to 'sealing'.

When the timer goes off, move the steam release handle to 'venting' to release the steam immediately. Ensure the carrots are soft all the way through by piercing the carrots with a fork.

Mix together the marinade ingredients either in a square tupperware container or in a large zip-loc bag. Place the carrots in with the marinade. Let them marinade for 12-24 hours. If using a tupperware container, you may want to flip the carrot dogs once.

When you are ready to eat them, take them out of the marinade and place them in your Instant Pot®. Pour in the marinade and hit the sautée button. Hit the adjust button so you get the 'high' temperature setting. Sautée for 10 minutes.

Serve the carrot dogs on your choice of oil-free hot dog buns and top with your favorite sauces.

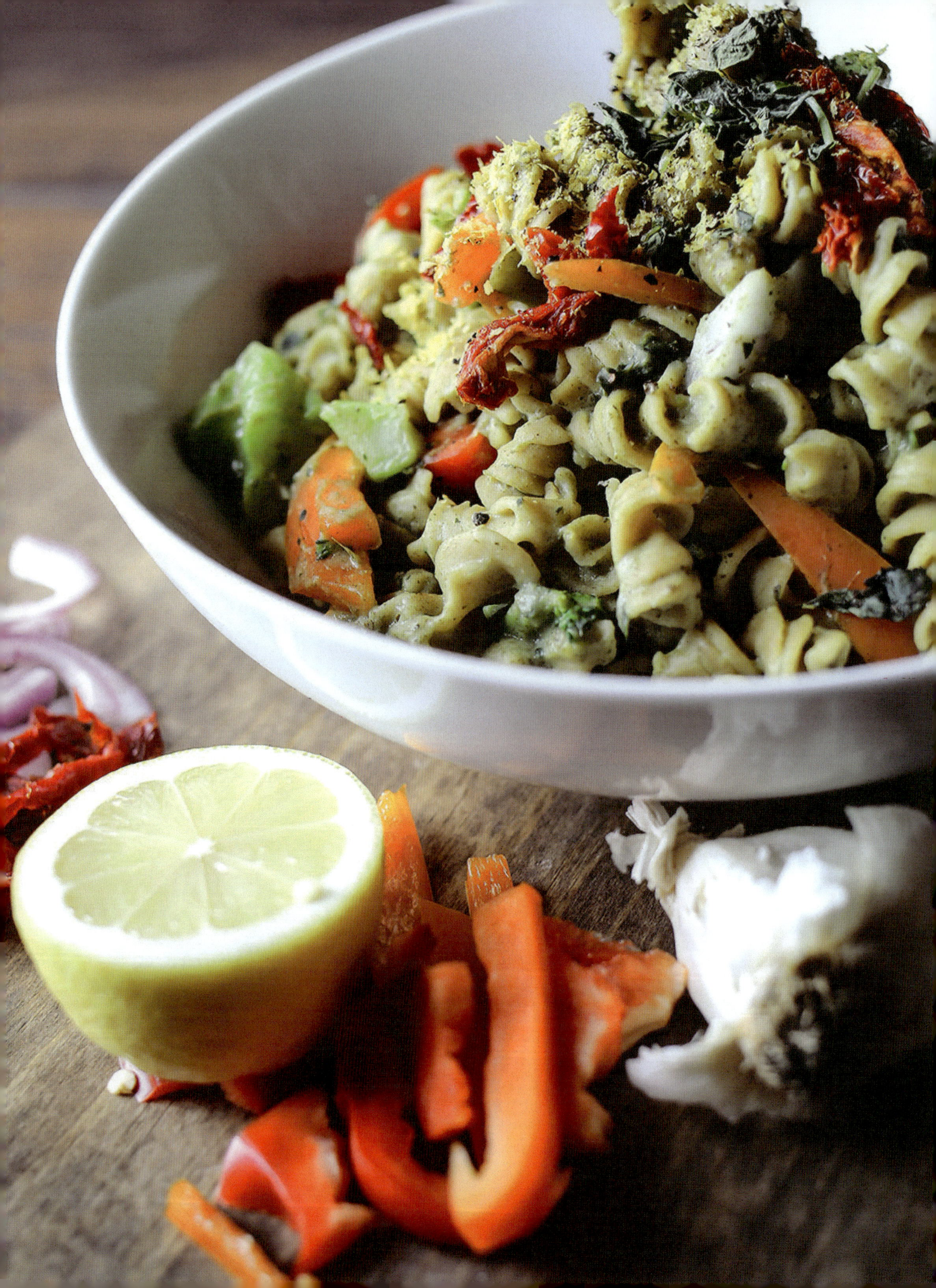

CREAMY ALFREDO PASTA

We love how versatile the Instant Pot® is. You can do so many wonderful dishes in there and this is one of them. Pasta like this is typically best eaten the same day if at all possible. It usually dries out if put in the fridge overnight.

SERVINGS	PREP TIME	TOTAL COOK TIME
3 x 600 calorie servings	10 minutes	25 minutes

INGREDIENTS

SAUCE
- 1 head of cauliflower
- 1/2 cup of water
- 4 garlic cloves, minced
- 1/4 cup of nutritional yeast
- 1 cup of spinach (frozen or fresh)
- 1/2 cup of artichoke hearts
- 1 lemon juiced (about 3 tbsp)
- 2 tsp salt

PASTA
- 1 lb (454g) of dry whole wheat fusilli pasta
- 3 1/2 cups of water

GARNISH
- Chopped red pepper
- Red onion
- Nutritional yeast
- Basil

METHOD

Cut the cauliflower in to 4 pieces. Place in iPot on the trivet. Add 1 1/2 cups of water. Hit pressure cook for 2 minutes. When the time is up release the pressure immediately.

Prepare the garlic, nutritional yeast, spinach, artichoke hearts, lemon juice and salt in a blender.

When the cauliflower is finished cooking, add it in to the blender. Blend all the ingredients together. Clean out the inner pot (will have some water and cauliflower bits from earlier) and pour the dry pasta in to the clean inner pot.

Pour the spinach alfredo sauce over the dry pasta. Pour in the 3 1/2 cups of water, 1 cup at a time stirring after each cup is added. The water level should be at the top of the dry pasta level. If a few pieces are poking above the water level, that is fine.

Hit the pressure cook button and set for 6 minutes on high pressure. When the cooking time is finished, release the pressure immediately. Serve soon after since the pasta will still cook in the pot if left unattended. Add some of the garnish ingredients to the top and enjoy!

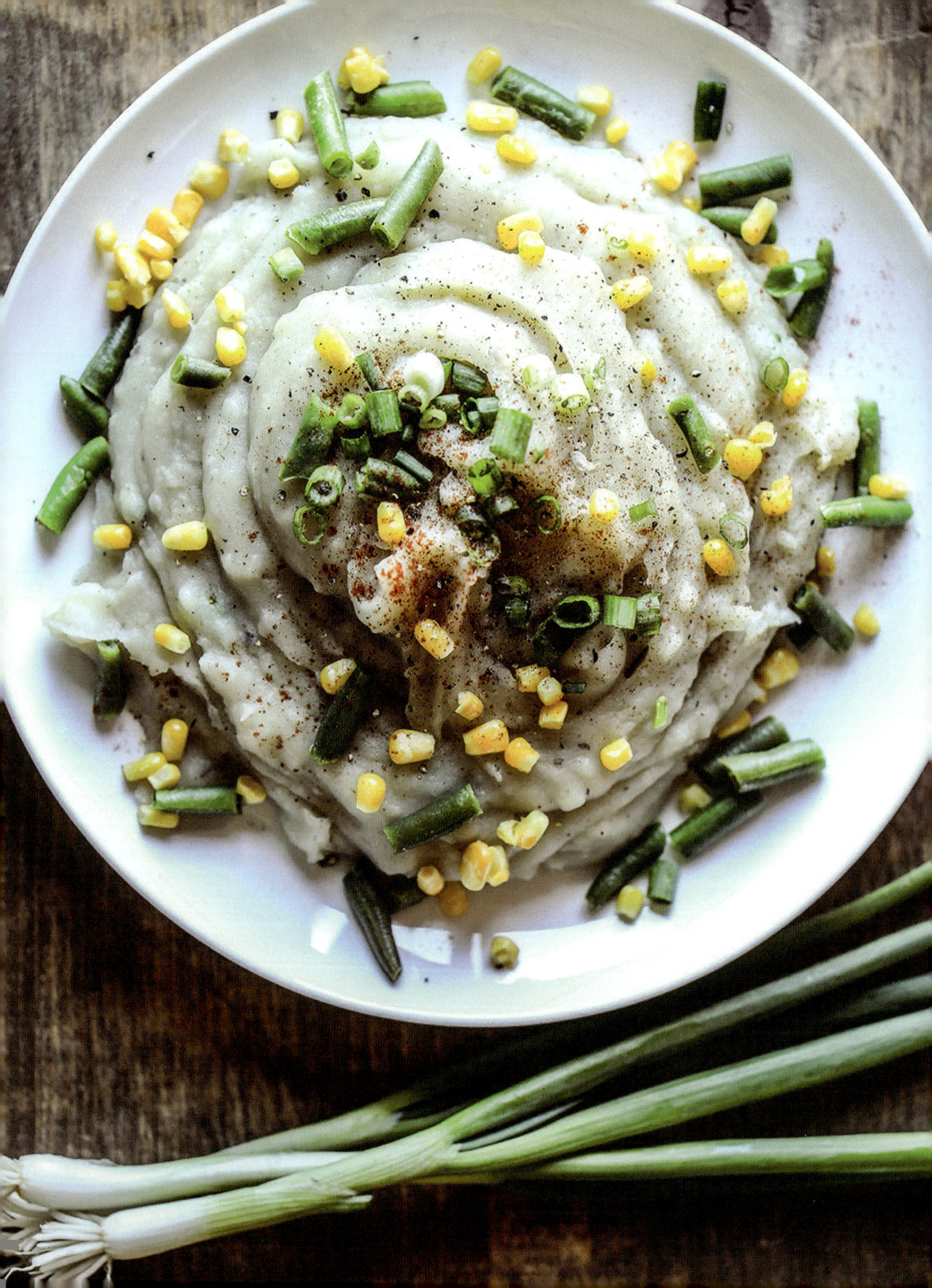

SMASHED POTATOES

Talk about the most ultimate comfort food. Who doesn't love some delicious smashed potatoes!?! This is a really simple method for some Quick And delcious smashed potatoes. Feel free to get creative and use different spices you prefer!

SERVINGS	PREP TIME	TOTAL COOK TIME
2 x 400 calorie servings	10 minutes	25 minutes

INGREDIENTS

SMASHED POTATOES
- 2 1/2 lbs (1250g) of potatoes, peeled and chopped
- 2 cups of water
- 1 tsp of salt
- 1/2 tsp of onion powder
- 1/2 tsp of garlic powder
- 1 tsp of Italian seasoning

GARNISH
- 1/2 cup of corn
- 1/2 cup of green beans
- 1 stalk of green onion, sliced

** Many people like to use different plant-based milks to add to their mashed potatoes. We found with this method in the Instant Pot®, we got a great consistency and taste just using water. But try the plant milk, it can take things to a whole new level!

METHOD

Alright, first thing you want to do is peel and chop all of your potatoes. For certain recipes we will give you a specific potato amount instead of a vague measurement like: 4 medium potatoes. That's just so that the potato:water ratio will be very similar to the one we used so you get optimal mashed potatoes.

Add the potatoes, salt, onion powder, garlic powder and Italian seasoning to your Instant Pot®. Sprinkle the seasonings over top to get an even coating. Add the water and use a spoon to mix the potatoes around.

Put the lid on. Place the Instant Pot® on pressure cook and set the time to 10 minutes on high pressure. Make sure the steam release handle is set to 'sealing'.

Once the Instant Pot® is finished cooking, let it naturally release for 10 minutes. Use the steam release handle to release the remaining steam. With the potatoes still in the iPot, use an immersion blender to blend the potatoes until you get the desired consistency.

Top with some optional corn, green beans and green onions.

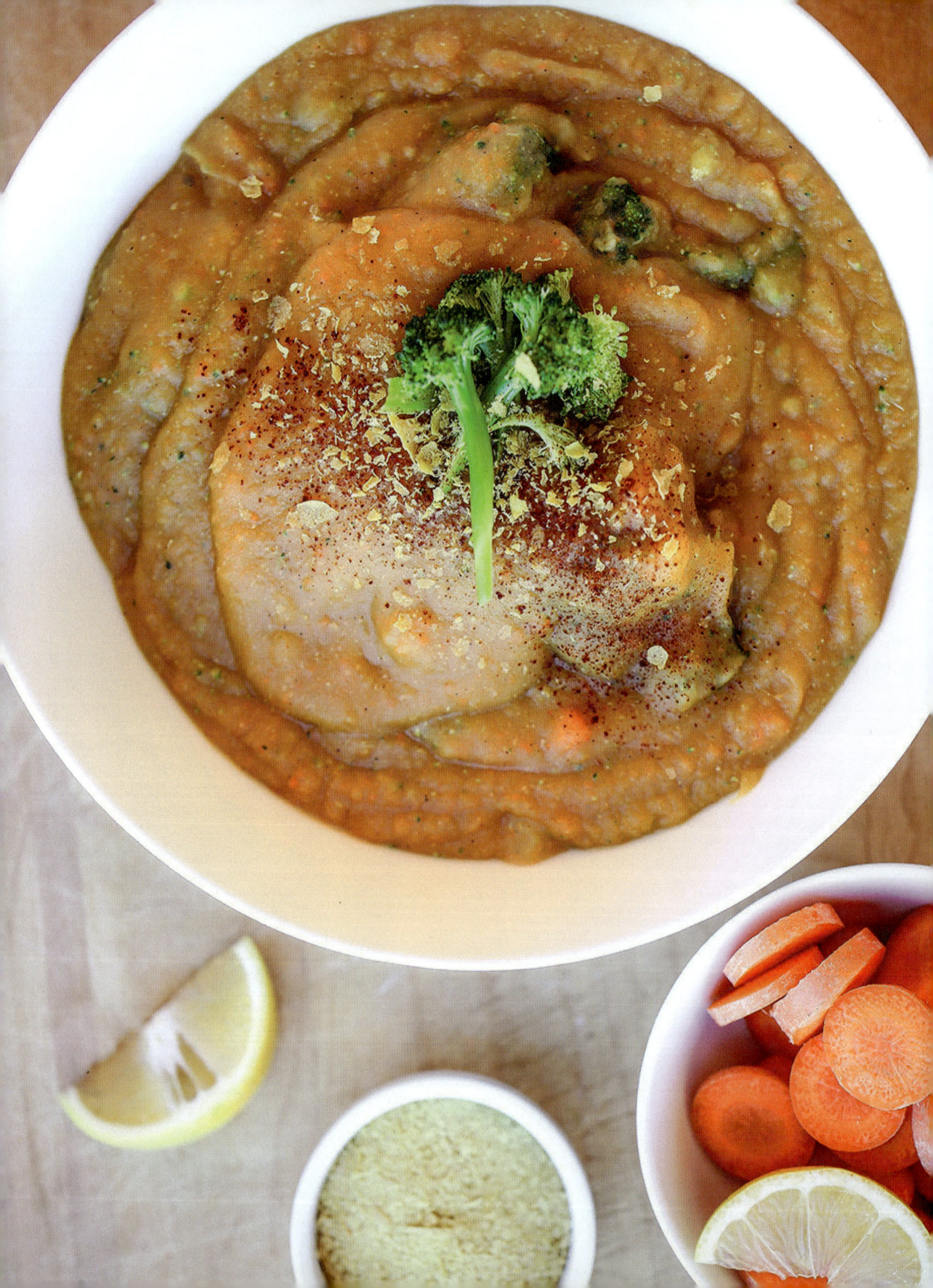

CHEESY POTATO BROCCOLI SOUP

Oh baby, this soup is really good! We really wanted to recreate a cheddar broccoli soup and we think we came really close! This another super healthy, low fat soup that really tastes bomb diggity. loving your Instant Pot® yet? We hope so!

SERVINGS	PREP TIME	TOTAL COOK TIME
2 x 440 calorie servings	10 minutes	30 minutes

INGREDIENTS

- 2 1/2 lb (1250g) of potatoes, peeled and chopped
- 1 broccoli head, chopped
- 3 carrots, chopped
- 4 cups of water
- 2 tsp salt
- 1/2 tsp smoked paprika
- 2 tsp chili powder *(½ chilli)*
- 1 tsp of garlic powder
- 1 tsp of turmeric
- 1/3 cup of nutritional yeast
- 1/2 of a lemon squeezed

METHOD

Place the head of broccoli on the trivet in the iPot with 1 cup of water poured in. Put the lid on, hit the pressure cook button and set the timer for 3 minutes. Once it is finished, release the steam immediately. Remove the broccoli, chop in to small bits and clean the inner pot for the next step.

Peel and chop the potatoes and add them in to the Instant Pot®. Add the chopped carrots and the remaining ingredients except for the nutritional yeast and lemon juice. We'll add those 2 ingredients in when the soup is finished cooking.

Set the Instant Pot® on pressure cook for 10 minutes on high pressure. Make sure the steam release handle is set to 'sealing'. Once the time is up, let it naturally release for 10 minutes and switch the handle to 'venting' to release the remaining steam.

Take your immersion blender and blend the soup completely so it is smooth. Add in the nutritional yeast and lemon juice and blend it once more quickly. Add in more water if you want a thinner consistency.

Add in the chopped broccoli at this point and just mix around with a spoon and you are ready to serve this!

FARMER'S MARKET
GOOD FOR YOU
GOOD FOR THE WORLD
ORGANIC
Pumpkin
BPA FREE LINER*
NET WT. 15 OZ. (425g)
USDA

PUMPKIN STEEL CUT OATS

We were totally suprised with how well this recipe turned out. I'm (Derek) totally a fan of steel cut oats. The texture just seems to be a bit more solid and chewy (in a good way) compared to a big pile of mush aka quick oats.

SERVINGS	PREP TIME	TOTAL COOK TIME
1 serving at 740 calories	5 minutes	25 minutes

INGREDIENTS

- 1 cup of steel cut oats
- 1 2/3 cups of water
- 1 frozen banana
- 3 medjool dates, chopped
- 1/2 cup of pumpkin purée
- 1 tbsp of coconut flakes
- 1 tbsp of buckwheat groats

METHOD

Ok here you go. This one is really easy.

Pour the cup of steel cut oats in to your Instant Pot®. Followed by the water, frozen banana, pumpkin purée and chopped dates.

Stir it around a little bit to get the pumpkin purée mixed in a bit. Make sure the steam release handle is set to 'sealing'. Set the Instant Pot® on pressure cook for 10 minutes.

Once the time is finished, let it naturally release for 10 minutes. Hit the 'Cancel' button and move the steam release handle to 'venting'.

Take a spoon and mix all that delicious goodness around. Since the banana and dates are cooked so well, they should just mash together with the oatmeal.

Top with some coconut flakes and buckwheat groats.

Enjoy!

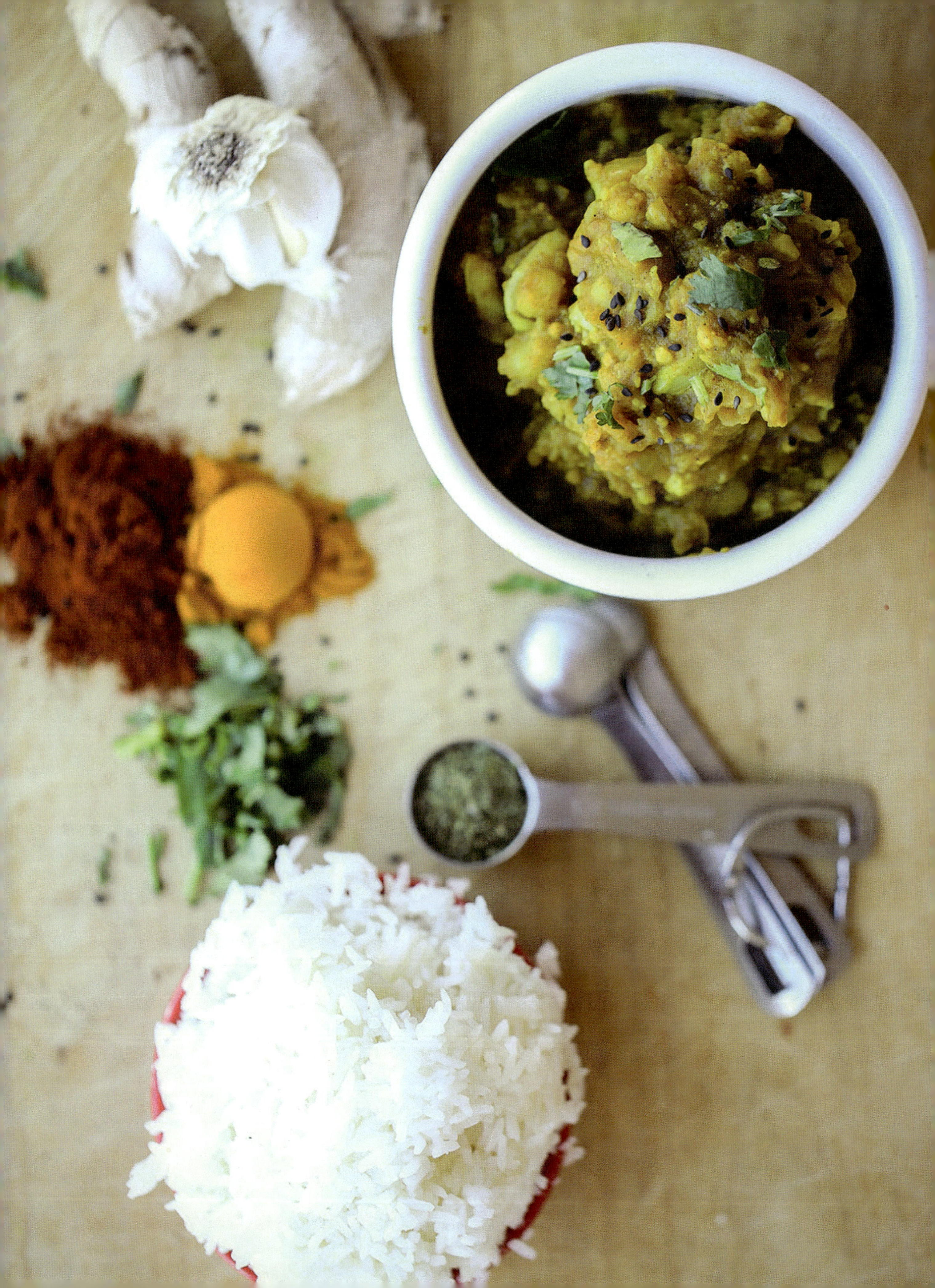

AMAZING ALOO GOBI

Everytime I've been to an indian buffet or restaurant, I've always loved the aloo gobi. So it has been in the back of my mind to recreate this at home using no oil but still have lots of flavor!

SERVINGS	PREP TIME	TOTAL COOK TIME
2 x 280 calorie servings	10 minutes	30 minutes

INGREDIENTS

- 1 1/2 lbs (675g) of potatoes, peeled and chopped
- 1 head of cauliflower
- 1 medium red onion, finely chopped
- 2 cups of water
- 3 cloves of garlic, minced
- 1 tsp of salt
- 1 tsp of garam masala
- 1 tsp of ground coriander
- 1/2 tsp of turmeric
- 1 tsp of chili powder
- 1 thumbnail of grated ginger

Handwritten notes:
- Tried:
- brussels also
- 4 cup water
- Did not steam cauli before
- half tsp cumin

METHOD

Steam the whole head of cauliflower for 2 minutes on the trivet with 1 1/2 cups of water. Immediately release the steam and use oven gloves to pull the trivet out of the iPot. Let it cool. Empty the Instant Pot® of water.

Sautée (using the sautée function) the finely chopped onions, grated ginger and minced garlic for 5 minutes with 1/2 cup of water. Once the time is up, hit the 'Cancel' button. Add in the 1 1/2 cups of water to the inner pot. Add in the chopped potatoes and spices. Mix it all around with a large spoon.

Put the lid on and set the Instant Pot® to pressure cook for 8 minutes on high pressure. Remember to set the steam release handle to 'sealing'. Once the Instant Pot® has finished cooking, let it naturally release for about 5-10 minutes. During this time, chop the cauliflower in to bit sized bits. It will be very soft and should be cooled down by now.

Use the steam release handle to release any extra steam after the 5-10 minutes is up and add in the cauliflower bits and mix around with a spoon.

This goes great over jasmine or basmati rice!

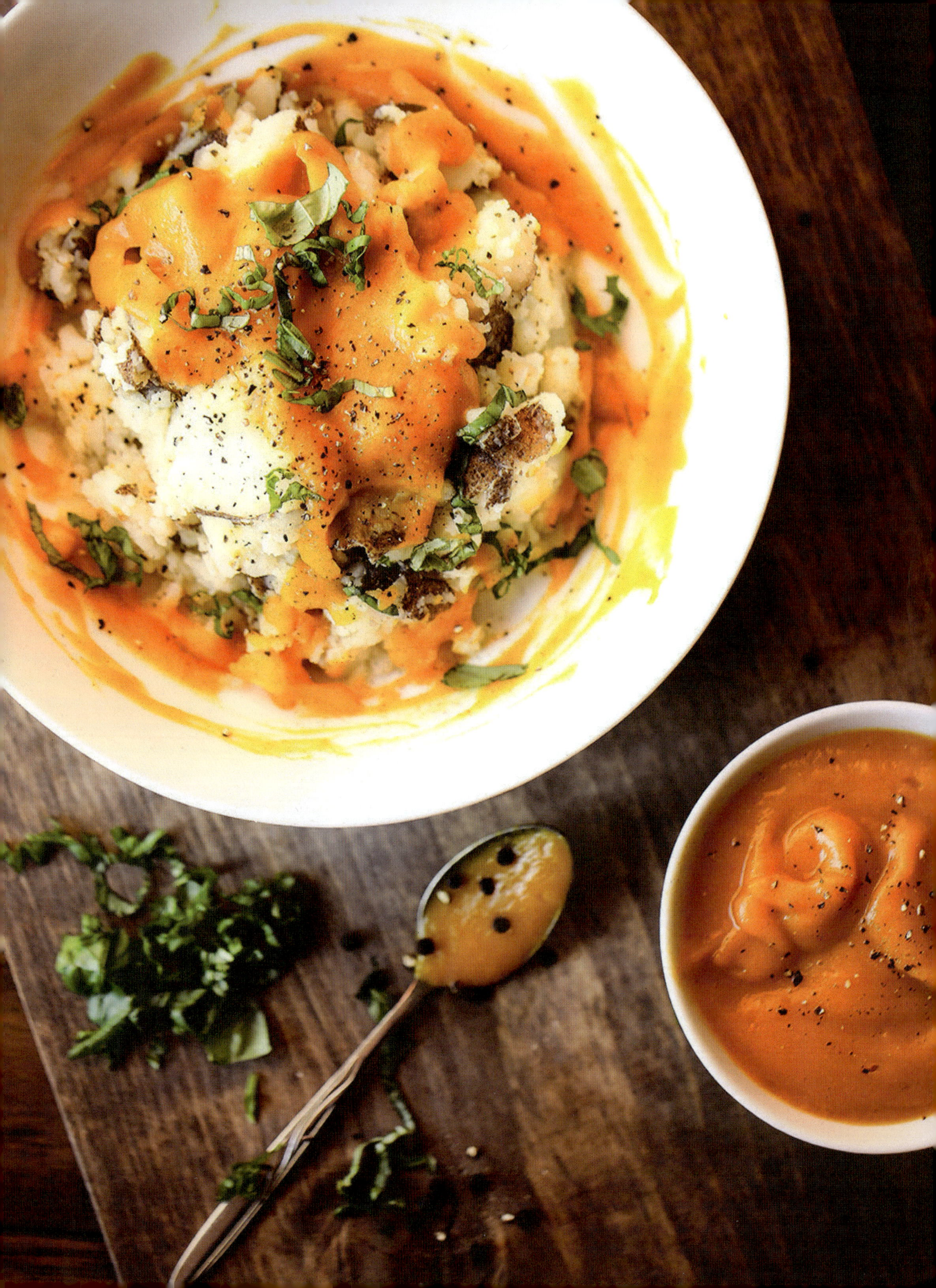

CARROT POTATO GRAVY

We can't get enough of this stuff. Yes, there is a lot of seasoning in it. It's meant to have a lot of flavor so you don't need a lot of it. Goes great on mashed potatoes or whatever else you're eating!

SERVINGS	PREP TIME	TOTAL COOK TIME
Makes about 2 cups of gravy	5 minutes	15 minutes

INGREDIENTS

- 1/2 lb (225g or about 4 medium) of carrots, chopped
- 1 small potato, (1/2 lb or 225g) peeled & chopped
- 2 cups of water
- 1 tsp of onion powder
- 1 tsp of garlic powder
- 1 tsp of salt
- 1/2 tsp of turmeric
- 2 tsp of soy sauce
- 2 tbsp of nutritional yeast

METHOD

Peel and chop your potato. Chop your carrot. Throw them both in to the Instant Pot® along with the water.

For this recipe we're going to add in all the spices and seasonings when the Instant Pot® is finished cooking. Put the lid on. Make sure the steam release handle is set to 'sealing' and set it to pressure cook for 7 minutes on high-pressure.

When the time is complete, let it naturally release steam for about 5 minutes then swith the handle to 'venting' to release the remaining steam.

At this point you have two options. Either take the cooked carrot potato mush and add it to a blender with the remaining ingredients and blend it.

You can also add in the remaining ingredients in to the Instant Pot® and use an immersion blender to make the gravy directly in the iPot.

If you want a thinner gravy then just add a touch more water.

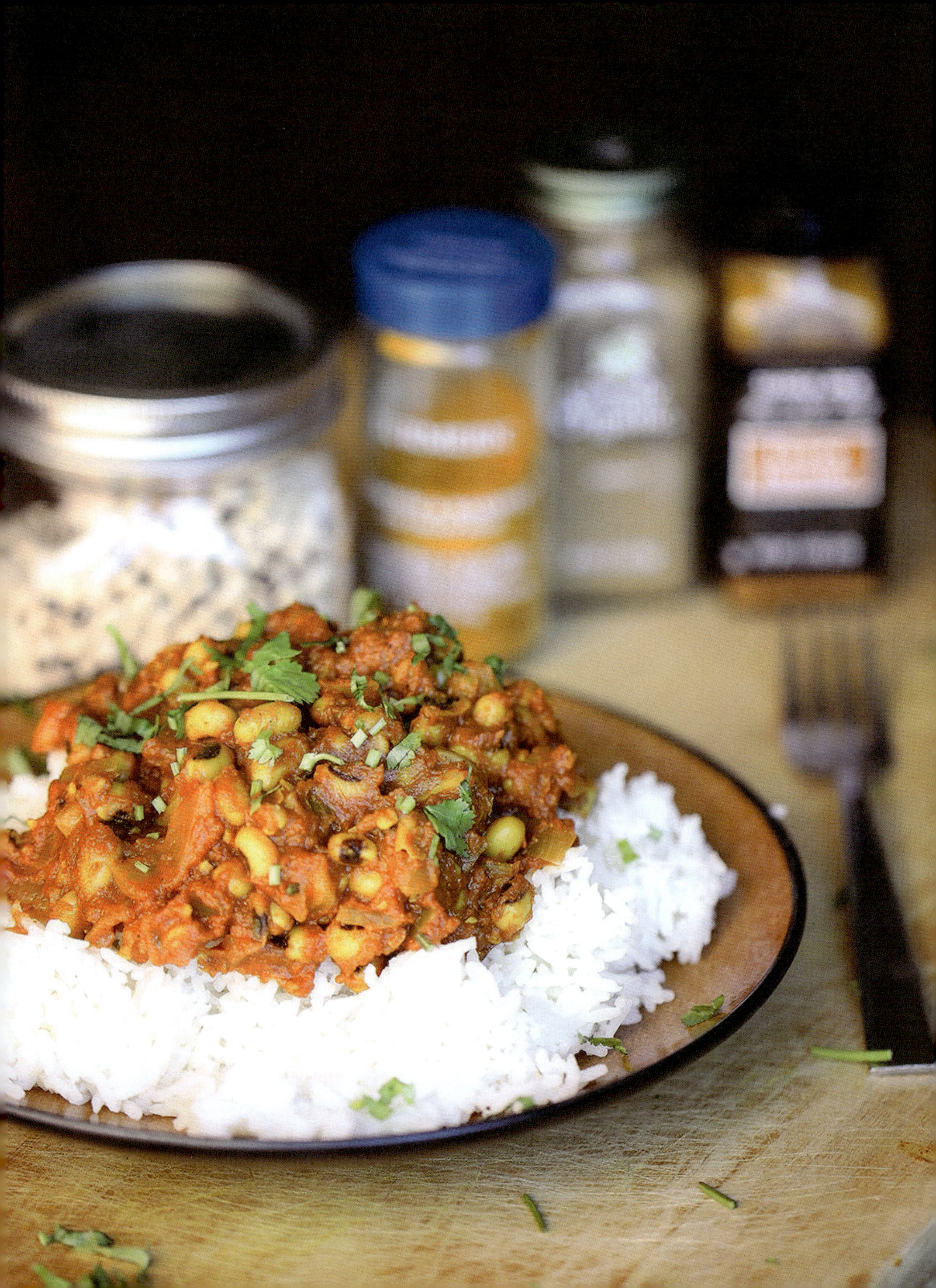

THE BLACK EYED PEAS CHILI

We asked the Black eyed peas if we could use their name in a recipe. Again we got a 'WTF' response back. Fergie wasn't having it... whatevs.

SERVINGS	PREP TIME	TOTAL COOK TIME
2 x 350 calorie servings	10 minutes	30 minutes

INGREDIENTS

- 1 1/2 cups of dry black eyed peas
- 4 cups of water
- 1 thumbnail of ginger, grated
- 3 cloves of garlic, minced
- 1 1/2 cups (1 small) of red onion, finely diced
- 15 oz can of tomato sauce (different from tomato paste or diced tomatoes)
- 1/2 tsp of curry powder
- 1/2 tsp of salt
- 1 tsp of cumin
- 1 tsp of garam masala
- 1/2 tsp of turmeric

METHOD

First thing you want to do is rinse and sort through 1 1/2 cups of the black eyed peas. Put in the Instant Pot® with 4 cups of water, put the lid on and set to pressure cook and high-pressure for 6 minutes. Once finished, let it naturally release for 10 minutes. Take the peas and drain the water using a colander. Set the peas aside in another container.

Wash the inner pot and add in the ginger, garlic and red onion along with 1/2 cup of water. Hit the sautée button (hit the adjust button twice so it goes to 'low' heat) and let it sautée for 5 minutes or until the onions are translucent. Keep stirring.

Add in the turmeric and garam masala and let it sautée for about 1 minute while stirring. Add in the tomato sauce, cumin, curry powder and black eyed peas. Let this sautée for another 2-3 minutes while stirring.

Remove the inner pot from the iPot and set on cutting board since it will be very hot. Add in the salt and give it one more stir.

This goes great alongside rice. Enjoy!

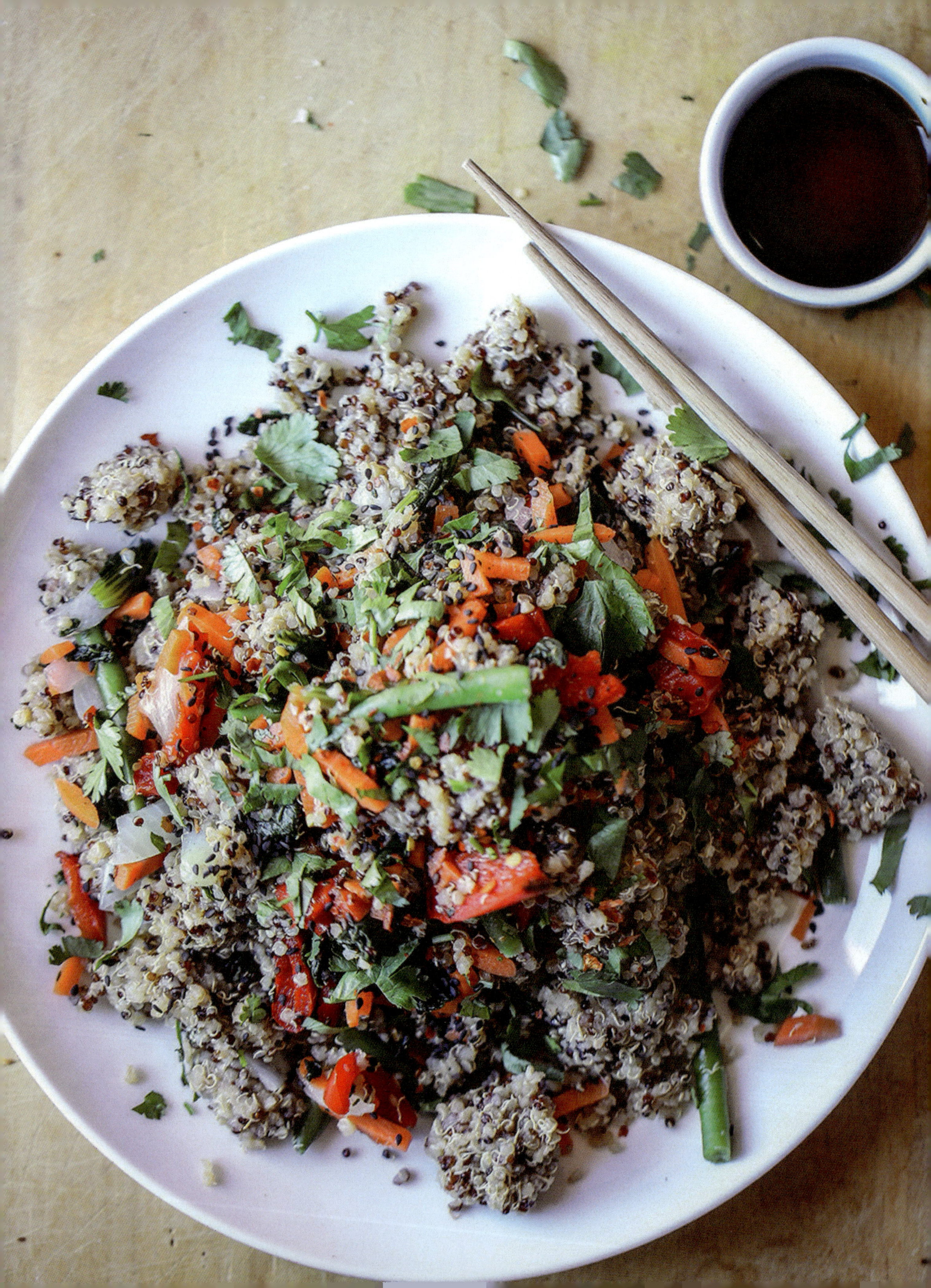

ASIAN STYLE QUINOA

Quinoa is one of those awesome ancient grains. It was domesticated 3,000 - 4,000 years ago for human consumption. It is packed with lots of protein and guess what? You can also do it in the Instant pot as well. Enjoy this tasty meal!

SERVINGS	PREP TIME	TOTAL COOK TIME
2 x 700 calorie servings	5 minutes	15 minutes

INGREDIENTS

- 2 cups of quinoa
- 4 cups of water
- 3 cloves of garlic, minced
- 2 tbsp soy sauce
- 2 tbsp of rice vinegar
- 2 tbsp of sugar
- 1 thumb of grated ginger
- 8 oz bag of Asian style frozen vegetables

METHOD

This is another one of those simple one pot recipes that takes almost no time at all!

If you have some forethought with this recipe, you can let the frozen vegetables thaw out before you cook this. We use this method and just added the veggies in after it was finished cooking so the more delicate veggies didn't get super soft and damaged for the photo.

So if you want to do it like that, here is how we made it. Combine all of the ingredients (except for frozen veggies) in to your Instant Pot. Put the lid on. Make sure the steam release handle is set to 'sealing' and set the iPot to 1 minute on pressure cook at high pressure. Yes! Only 1 minute.

Once the cooking time is finished, let it naturally release for 10 minutes. Move the steam release handle to 'venting' to release the remaining steam. Remove the lid. Then add in the thawed frozen vegetables and mix around.

If the frozen veggies aren't thawed, just add it in with the rest of ingredients at the beginning.

Enjoy!

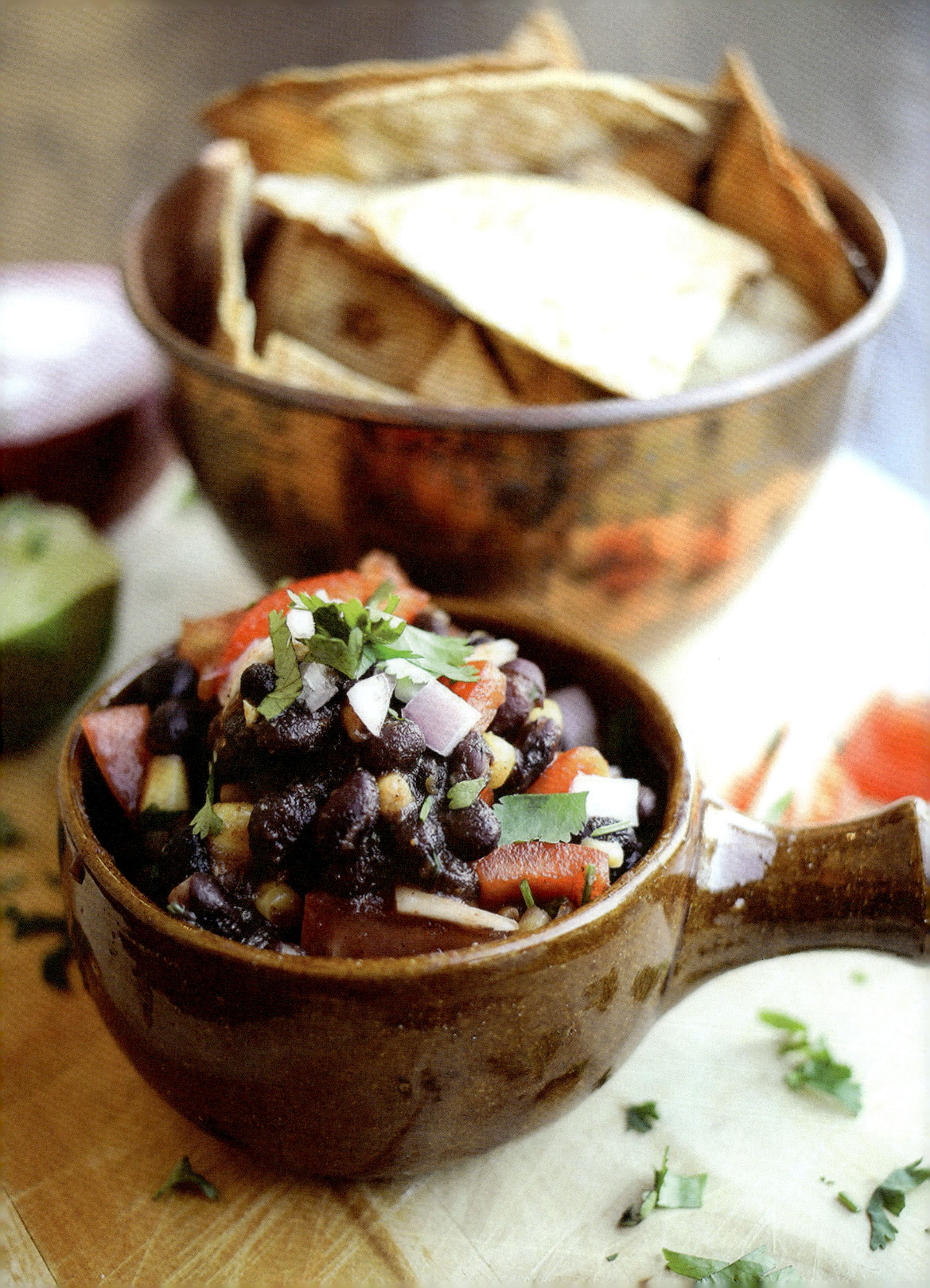

THE 7 DAY CHALLENGE
(ONLY FOR THE COURAGEOUS, TAKE YOUR INSTANT POTTING TO THE NEXT LEVEL)

WHY DO THIS CHALLENGE?

One of the things that we absolutely love with the Instant Pot is that you can use it at every meal. It isn't one of those appliances that you use once in a blue moon. We literally use ours every day. We choose to live minimally and since this gets so much use, it has become a valuable tool in our life to make great tasting food fast and easily.

We recommend the iPot so highly because of how useful it is. Especially for people that don't really like to cook. It is so easy to throw some ingredients in to the iPot, hit a few buttons and that's all you have to do. Since you're cooking in large batches, you will most definitely have leftovers that you can bring to work or school.

We wanted to make a 7 day challenge so that we could challenge you to use your Instant Pot to cook every meal for a week. Why not eh!

The point with this challenge is to get you comfortable using the iPot and using different ingredients that maybe you wouldn't normally use. You can gain greater confidence in the kitchen so that making healthy plant-based meals becomes second nature to you.

Keep in mind that the 7 day challenge will have to be adapted to you and your caloric needs. Someone doing this challenge may only require 1800 calories a day and someone else may need 3000 calories. We've based the meals to give you about 2000-2400 calories per day which is a good happy medium for most adults.

Focus on eating till you're satisfied and if you need more or less, you will know for the next time you use your iPot.

Remember to try out as many recipes in this book as possible. They're all so good and good for you.

Good luck!

Derek & Hannah

SHOPPING GUIDE

STARCHES & GRAINS

8 cups (3 1/2 lbs) of jasmine rice
2 cups (2/3 lb or 360g) of steel cut oats
1 cup (1/4 lb or 100g) of quick oats
2 cups (2/3 lb or 340g) of quinoa

FRUITS & VEGETABLES

7 lbs (3.2kg) of potatoes
1 1/2 lb (700g or about 12 medium) of carrots
3 bananas (2 to be frozen)
6 medjool dates
15 oz (450mL) can of pumpkin purée
1 cup of frozen berries
1 can (14.5 fl oz or 429mL) of diced tomatoes
2 cans (6 oz or 170g) of tomato paste
1 head of broccoli
1 lemon
1 lime
1 cup of frozen mango chunks
8 oz (225g) of Asian frozen vegetables
1 red pepper
1 yellow pepper
3 medium sized tomatoes
1 bunch of celery
1 cup of fresh or frozen corn
2 1/2 large yellow onions
1/4 cup of cilantro
bunch of green onion

BEANS & LEGUMES

1 1/2 cups (2/3 lb or 300g) of dry pinto beans
3 cups (1 1/2 lbs or 680g) of dry red lentils
2 cups (1 lb or 454g) of green split peas

SPICES & CONDIMENTS

3 tbsp of chili powder
2 tbsp of cumin
1 1/2 tsp smoked paprika
2 tsp of cayenne pepper
1 tsp of Italian seasoning
1 1/2 tsp of onion powder
2 1/2 tsp of garlic powder
2 1/2 tbsp of soy sauce
2 tbsp of rice vinegar
1/4 cup of red wine vinegar
6 tsp of salt
1 1/2 tsp of turmeric
3/4 cup of brown sugar
12 tsp of Better Than Bouillon
1 tsp of liquid smoke
2 tbsp of sriracha (optional)

OTHER

1/4 cup soy milk or almond milk
2 cups of sweetened coconut milk
2 tbsp of coconut flakes
2 tbsp of buckwheat groats
1 cup of salsa
7 oz of herdez mexican salsa (see the chapter 'Ingredients We Use')
4 oz (80mL) can of diced jalapeños
1/2 cup of nutritional yeast
black seasame seeds (optional)
16 cloves of garlic
1 thumb of ginger
1/2 tsp of ground black pepper
1/4 cup of oil-free bread crumbs
4 oil-free hamburger buns

LET'S DO THIS!!

DAY 0

If you were to do this challenge from Monday to Sunday, this would be the Sunday before Monday. This is a great day to get your shopping done plus you can get a few meals made before you start the week.

Recipes To Make:
DMAN'S EPIC REFRIED BEANS (PAGE 29)
CARROT POTATO GRAVY (PAGE 75)
1 CUP OF STEAMED RICE (PAGE 21)

Take about 1/3 of the refried beans and place in a tupperware container with the steamed rice. Add about 1/2 cup of salsa. Place this in the fridge and now you have lunch for tomorrow ready.

DAY 1

Breakfast
PUMPKIN STEEL CUT OATS (PAGE 71)
Today's the first day! Let's start the day off right with some delicious pumpkin steel cut oats.

Lunch
STEAMED RICE WITH BEANS & SALSA (WHAT YOU MADE ON DAY 0)

Dinner
SMASHED POTATOES WITH CARROT GRAVY (PAGE 67)
You'll only need about 1/2 of the smashed potato recipe.
Reserve the rest of it for lunch tomorrow.

~ 7 DAY CHALLENGE MEAL PLAN ~

DAY 2 ....

Breakfast
OMG BERRY OATMEAL (PAGE 27)
Alright, Day 2. Let's do this!

Lunch
SMASHED POTATOES WITH CARROT GRAVY
For lunch have the Smashed Potatoes that you made for dinner yesterday and top with some of that delicious Carrot Gravy.

Dinner
PROTEIN LENTIL STEW (PAGE 35) AND 1 CUP OF DRY RICE
Once you make this, you'll probably have enough of it for days. You'll only need 1 to 2 cups of it when you're eating it with rice. Make 3 dry cups of rice. You'll only need 1 cup of rice for dinner, the other 2 cups will be for tomorrow.

DAY 3 ....

Breakfast
1 CUP OF DRY RICE WITH REFRIED BEANS
Use half of the leftover rice from last night's dinner (or you'll need to cook another 2 cups for today). Top the rice with the refried beans, some salsa or any other condiments you love.

Lunch
LENTIL STEW AND 1 CUP OF DRY RICE
Combine 1 or 2 cups of the lentil stew from last night with 1 dry cup of rice. We love to put hot sauce on top of ours for some extra zing! Leave some of the lentil stew for Day 5.

Dinner
CHEESY POTATO BROCCOLI SOUP (PAGE 69)
Tired of rice? Well let's get some delicious potato recipes in to your belly. Let's make the cheesy broccoli potato soup for dinner tonight. Eat half of it and pack away the rest of it for work or school tomorrow.

~ 7 DAY CHALLENGE MEAL PLAN ~

DAY 4

Breakfast
MANGO STICKY RICE (PAGE 41)
For breakfast make some of that delicious mango sticky rice. This was such an awesome treat both of us have had while traveling overseas. You can make a smaller version of this recipe by using 2/3 cup of dry rice and 1 cup of coconut milk.

Lunch
CHEESY BROCCOLI POTATO SOUP (FROM DAY 3)
Do you notice a trend of your lunch being what you had for dinner the night previous? This is great for people who work and go to school so that you can always have a healthy meal to eat.

Dinner
ASIAN STYLE QUINOA (PAGE 79)
For tonight, we'll switch it up to another delicious grain. Quinoa is packed full of protein and this recipe is super tasty. Eat half of the recipe for dinner and save the other half for lunch tomorrow.

DAY 5

Breakfast
LENTIL STEW (FROM DAY 2) AND 1 CUP OF DRY RICE
You should still have some of the lentil stew leftover. Steam 1 cup of dry rice and eat along with the lentil stew.

Lunch
ASIAN STYLE QUINOA (FROM DAY 4)
Guess what's for lunch today! More dinner from yesterday!

Dinner
BLACK BEAN SOUP OF GLORY (PAGE 47) AND RICE OR POTATOES
If you're doing this challenge from Monday to Sunday then today is Friday! Let loose with the Black Bean Soup. No really… that's how we party in our household at least. Match up a few cups of the soup along with either some steamed diced potatoes or steamed rice. Save some of the bean soup for tomorrow as well!

~ 7 DAY CHALLENGE MEAL PLAN ~

DAY 6

Breakfast
PUMPKIN STEEL CUT OATS (PAGE 71)
We don't feel weird eating 'dinner' food for breakfast. We don't discriminate the time of day. If you're one of those that feel off, make the pumpkin steel cut oats again for breakfast. They're really good!

Lunch
BLACK BEAN SOUP (FROM DAY 5)
Steam 1 cup of dry rice and serve that alongside the Black Bean Soup you made yesterday.

Dinner
SPLIT 'EM UP PEA SOUP (PAGE 61)
Ever remember your Mom making you pea soup? Well I do! Not cut up hotdogs in this pea soup though. Just the straight goodness.

DAY 7

Breakfast
PERFECTLY STEAMED POTATOES (PAGE 23)
For many of you, today will be Sunday. Time to let loose. Steam 1 to 1 1/2 lbs of potatoes. Any kind you want. Once they are finished, place the potatoes on a plate and mash with a fork. Top with some salt, salsa, green onion and 1 medium tomato. Gobble this delicious mash up! This is even something you can make most mornings as well.

Lunch
THE SLOPPIEST JOE YOU'LL EVER KNOW (PAGE 55)
A Sunday lunch without Sloppy Joes just doesn't feel right. Reward your Instant Pot prowess with a couple of these bad boys. If you follow the recipe you'll have some Sloppy Joe mix leftover along with some buns so you already have a meal prepared for day 8!

Dinner
SPLIT 'EM UP PEA SOUP (FROM DAY 6) AND 1 CUP OF DRY RICE
Final meal of the challenge. Remember what you had for dinner last night? Well you're having it again. Serve this alongside 1 cup of dry rice.

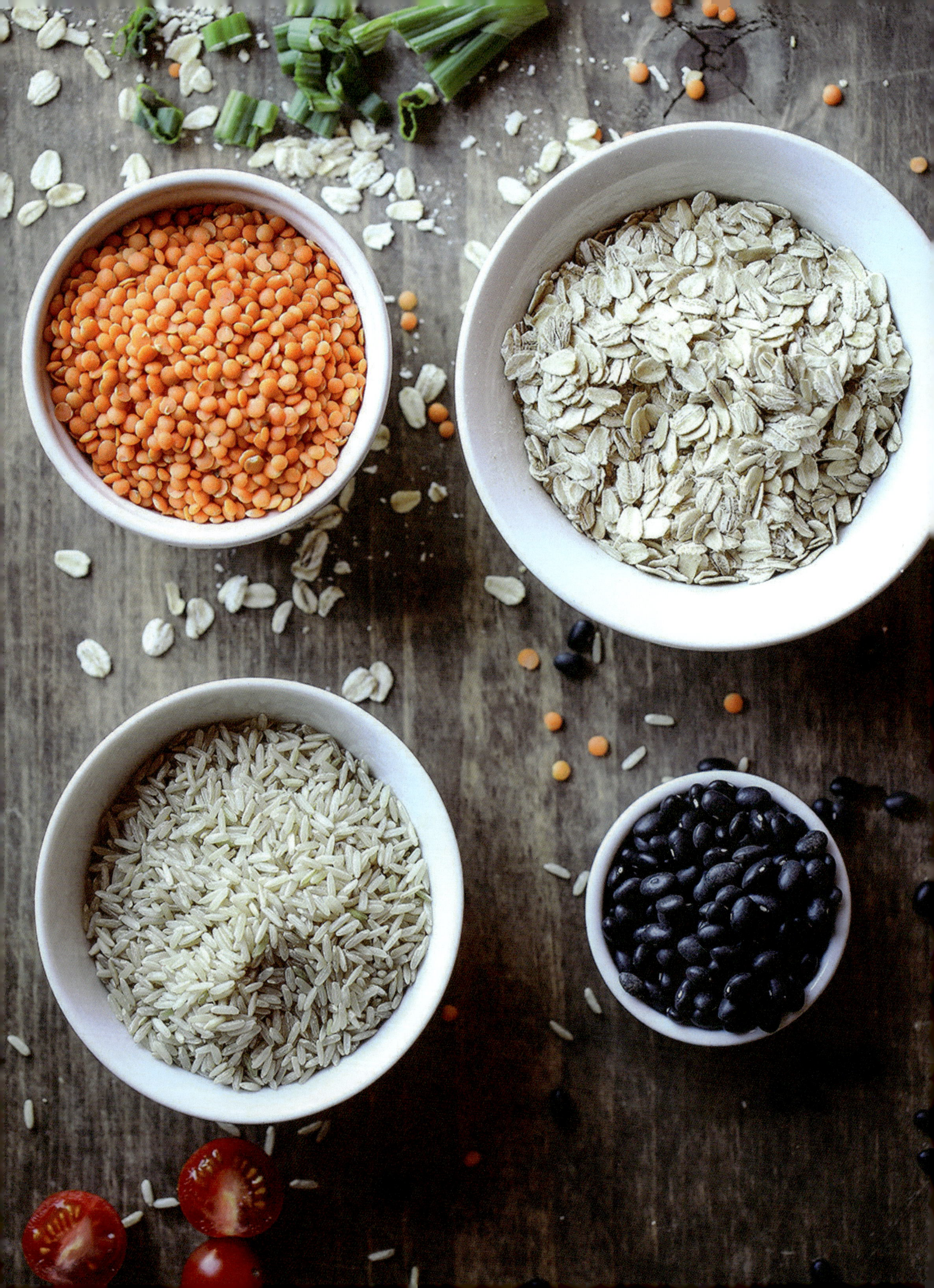

COOKING CHARTS

(IF YOU WANNA COOK SOME OTHER STUFF UP)

~ COOKING CHARTS ~

RICE & GRAINS

All cooking times are at high pressure and use a 10 minute natural release. Never fill your Instant Pot® more than 1/2 way with either grains or beans plus the cooking liquid. They need room to expand inside the iPot.

Rice & Grains	Grain : Water Ratio	Cooking Time
Rice, Jasmine	1 : 1	4
Rice, Brown	1 : 1 1/4	22
Rice, Basmati	1 : 1 1/2	4
Rice, Wild	1 : 3	25
Oats, Quick	1 : 1 2/3	6
Oats, Steel Cut	1 : 1 2/3	10
Quinoa	1 : 2	1
Millet	1 : 1 1/2	1
Barley, pearl	1 : 2	20
Barley, whole	1 : 2 1/4	35

~ COOKING CHARTS ~

DRY BEANS & LEGUMES

All cooking times are at high pressure and Use A Full natural release. Whenever possible. let the pressure go down naturally for pressure cooking beans & Legumes since they generate a lot of foam and could spray out of the steam release handle if it is switched to venting immediately after cooking.

When cooking dried beans, use enough liquid to cover the beans plus two inches to the top level of the beans.

Beans & Legumes	Dry, Cook Time	Soaked, Cook Time
Pinto Beans	30	20
Black Beans	25	15
Navy Beans	20	15
Red Kidney Beans	24	15
Cannellini	40	20
Garbanzo Beans (Chickpeas)	40	25
Black Eyed Peas	7	N/A
Lentils	12	N/A
Split Lentils	1	N/A
Green Peas, Split	5	N/A
Green Peas, Whole	18	N/A

~ COOKING CHARTS ~

FRESH VEGETABLES

Place the veggies on your trivet and add the liquid to the bottom With all of the fresh vegetables on top of it. You want the veggies to be lifted out of the water. quickly release once the cooking time is finished (except for potatoes).

Fresh Vegetable	Size	Cook Time (minutes)	Cups Of Water
Artichokes	Whole	8-11	1 1/2
Asparagus	Whole or Cut	1	1
Beans, green	Whole or Cut	2-3	1
Beets (tops cut off)	Whole	15	2
Broccoli	Whole	3	1
Brussel Sprouts	Whole	2	1
Cabbage	2" chunks	2	1
Carrots	Whole	3	1 1/2
Cauliflower (remove outer leaves)	Whole Head	2	1 1/2
Celery	Whole	1	1
Corn	Cob	5	1
Eggplant	Slices or Chunks	3	1

～ COOKING CHARTS ～

Fresh Vegetable	Size	Cook Time (minutes)	Cups Of Water
Mixed Vegetables	Cubed	2	1
Okra	Whole or Cut	2-3	1
Onions	Whole	3	1
Parsnips	Chunks	2-3	1
Peas, green	Whole	1-2	1
Potatoes	Whole	15	2
Potatoes	Quartered	5	1
Pumpkin	Cubed & Peeled	4	1
Rutabaga	Cubed & Peeled	3	1
Squash, acorn	Cubed & Peeled	6	1 1/2
Squash, butternut	Cubed & Peeled	5	1 1/2
Squash, summer or yellow	Cubed & Peeled	2	1 1/2
Sweet Potato or Yams	Whole	10	2
Sweet Potato or Yams	Quartered	4	1
Turnips	Cubed & Peeled	3	1

Nacho 'Cheese' Dip from
LET'S GET SAUCY

OUR OTHER BOOKS

LET'S GET SAUCY
Over 55 mind blowing vegan sauce recipes!

highcarb.co/saucy

WEIGHT LOSS CHEAT SHEET
30 recipes + tons of info to get you started!

highcarb.co/cheatsheet

FREE!

LEAN & CLEAN EBOOK
14 day meal plan for maximum weight loss

highcarb.co/lean

PLANT APP
100s of recipes and customizable meal plans right in your pocket.

highcarb.co/app

HIGHCARBHANNAH.CO | EPIC VEGAN PRESSURE COOKING

Printed in Great Britain
by Amazon